Spelling

A Spelling Workbook with Comprehension Drills

Burton Goodman

Master the 320 Words Most Frequently Misspelled

New York, New York   Columbus, Ohio   Chicago, Illinois   Peoria, Illinois   Woodland Hills, California

Burton Goodman has taught English and reading in junior and senior high schools and in college for twenty-five years. He is the author of more than sixty language arts texts, and his short stories and articles have appeared in many national publications. He has written television scripts for Paramount Pictures and King Features Syndicate and wrote the Crafts and Culture segments for the acclaimed educational TV program "Vegetable Soup" for the Public Broadcasting System.

Mr. Goodman is the author of *Fist Against the Night,* a young adult novel that was published by the McGraw-Hill Companies. He is also the author of the following popular Jamestown series: *Goodman's Five-Star Stories, Goodman's Five-Star Activity Books,* and *English, YES!*

Photo Credits
9 Craig Lovell/CORBIS; **19** Jeff Schultz/Alaska Stock Images;
31 PhotoDisc; **41** Library of Congress; **53** Stock Montage/Newberry Library;
63 Cumberland County Museum; **75** Popperphoto/Archive Photos;
85 PhotoDisc

Glencoe/McGraw-Hill
A Division of The McGraw-Hill Companies

Send all inquiries to:
Glencoe/McGraw-Hill
8787 Orion Place
Columbus, OH 43240-4027

ISBN: 0-07-827356-0
Printed in the United States of America.

5 6 7 8 9 10 11 12 13 14 113 11 10 9 08 07 06

Contents

Unit 5: Literary Favorites

Unit 6: Strange Events

Unit 7: Olympic Feats

Unit 8: Safety First

To the Teacher

Five-Star Spelling has been specially designed to help your students master the 320 words that are most frequently misspelled. At the same time, it will help students build their reading power.

There are thirty-six lessons in *Five-Star Spelling*—about one for each week of the school year. If you wish, you may cover two lessons a week to complete the material during a single term. The book is organized into eight units, each of which contains four theme-related reading passages. A Cumulative Review appears after every other unit.

Each lesson begins with a carefully constructed high-interest reading passage. The passage provides a context for the spelling words and, simultaneously, affords opportunities for students to master five essential reading comprehension skills. Within each passage are ten of the most frequently misspelled words. The words are identified in boldface type. Each passage also contains an underlined word for vocabulary study.

Each lesson begins on a right-hand page. Following the reading passage are five questions to help your students build their reading POWER in five important comprehension skills areas. The questions always appear in the same order.

The questions provide your students with repeated practice in finding main ideas, recognizing details, defining unfamiliar words by using context clues, understanding cause-and-effect relationships, and drawing inferences. Students will

Pick the Main Idea

Observe Supporting Details

Watch for New Vocabulary

Explain Cause and Effect

Read to Draw Inferences

After the students have completed the Reading POWER portion of the lesson, they should write each of the ten boldface spelling words in a sentence in their notebooks. They should then be instructed to study the spelling of the words at home.

The way that students study spelling varies. There is no one best way. Research has shown that different methods prove effective for different students. Here is a list of common methods of studying spelling:

- Look carefully at the word.
- Write the word over and over.
- Divide the word into its syllables.
- Identify the difficult parts of the word and focus on them.
- See if a spelling rule applies—or does not apply—to the word.
- Find hints or clues in the word to help you remember its spelling.
- Say the word, and then spell it aloud.
- Close your eyes and visualize the word.
- Test yourself by covering the word and trying to spell it. Then uncover it to see if you are correct.
- Have someone test you on the words.
- Keep a list of the words you regularly misspell.
- Review the words often.

These methods are featured on page 103—Spelling Strategies. Encourage your students to refer to that page, to try each of the methods, and to choose the ones that work best for them.

On the left-hand page of each lesson is a section called Check Your Spelling Power. This section provides ten exercises designed to check and reinforce mastery of most of the frequently misspelled words introduced in that lesson *and* some frequently misspelled words from previous lessons. Your students should be aware that after they have studied the spelling words in a particular lesson, they must review *all* the words they have learned to that point.

Emphasize that through repeated study and review, they will eventually master all of the words that students frequently misspell.

The formats of the spelling checks vary. When you instruct the students to complete a Check Your Spelling Power exercise, tell them that they should do so without looking back at the passage. You may have the students correct the exercises on their own, using the answer key in the back of the book, or you may wish to correct the exercises as a class. Have students list in their notebooks the words that they misspell on the spelling checks. Encourage students to give those words special attention when they study.

Periodically, you may wish to give oral tests of the words the students have studied. For your convenience, all the words introduced in *Five-Star Spelling* are listed, by lesson number, on pages 101 and 102. A complete alphabetical list appears on page 104.

Following the spelling check in each lesson is a section called Words Often Confused and Misused. It contains an explanation of the distinctions between two or three words that are commonly confused and misused, examples of their correct use, and an exercise that requires the students to use the words. The students will learn both the meanings and the spellings of words like *except* and *accept*—words that are commonly used incorrectly. Students will be tested on these words in the Cumulative Reviews.

Five-Star Spelling offers a comprehensive and practical skills package for your students. By carefully and conscientiously doing each lesson in the book, they will systematically master the 320 words that are most frequently misspelled. Students will also learn to spell and understand the meanings of sixty-six words that are often confused and misused. At the same time, the special design of *Five-Star Spelling* will help your students build their reading power steadily and surely.

The lessons are not hard, but the groups of spelling words introduced in each high-interest passage do increase slightly in difficulty as the book progresses. However, if your students do each lesson carefully and review every week, they *will* master the words and become better spellers for life.

To the Student

Are there certain words that you always misspell? Maybe you can't remember if you should change the *y* to *i,* or if a consonant should be doubled, or if it's *ie* or *ei*? Well, you're not alone. There is a long list of words that many students have trouble remembering how to spell. But you can learn to spell those words once and for all. Help is on the way in this book.

Five-Star Spelling contains 320 words that students frequently misspell—and exercises to help you learn them. These troublesome words were identified by surveying lists of frequently misspelled words and "spelling demons" and by consulting with experts on spelling and with teachers of English. Yes, the 320 words in this book have been frequently misspelled. However, through study and review, you can master those words and become a much better speller.

This book also contains sixty-six words that students commonly confuse and misuse. Some examples are *its* and *it's, lose* and *loose,* and *stationary* and *stationery*. You will learn the differences in meaning between the words, as well as how to spell each one.

The program is not difficult. It simply requires effort and attention. If there's one key to success in spelling, it lies in repetition and review. By reviewing repeatedly, you plant the words firmly in your mind. After every eighth lesson, you will find a Cumulative Review. Each review contains exercises to help you check how well you have learned the words that have been presented up until that point in the book.

In addition, as you work your way through the book, you will increase your reading comprehension. Each of the thirty-two lessons begins with a brief, interesting reading passage followed by five reading comprehension questions. The questions will help you build your reading POWER as you

Pick the Main Idea

Observe Supporting Details

Watch for New Vocabulary

Explain Cause and Effect

Read to Draw Inferences

On the next page you will find directions that will help you work your way through the lessons. On page 103 is a list of tried-and-true ways to study spelling. Now you're on your way. Have fun! Good luck!

Burton Goodman

How to Complete a Lesson

- Read the passage carefully.
- Answer the five reading comprehension questions that follow the passage. Working with these questions will help you become a better reader.
- At your teacher's direction, check your answers to the reading comprehension questions. You may refer to the answer key at the back of the book.
- Look at and carefully study the ten boldface words in the reading passage. They are words that students often misspell. In your spelling notebook, write each of those words in a sentence. Underline the spelling word in each sentence.
- Study the spellings of the words at home. Be sure also to review *all* the words you studied in previous lessons. Concentrate especially on words you spelled incorrectly on the spelling check in each lesson. By reviewing the words repeatedly, you will eventually master them.
- Complete the Check Your Spelling Power section on the second page of the lesson. It contains most of the words from the reading passage in the lesson and some of the words from previous lessons. Check yourself without looking back at the passage.
- At your teacher's direction, check your answers, using the answer key at the back of the book.
- In your notebook, write the words you missed on the spelling check. (You should keep a running list of all the words you miss on the spelling checks.) Study and review these words until you master them.
- Complete the Words Often Confused and Misused section. This section teaches you the difference between words that look or sound alike but have different meanings. These words are commonly used incorrectly. You will learn the meanings of the words, as well as how to spell them. At your teacher's direction, check your answers.

Unit 1

Complicated Creatures

When you have completed this unit, you will have mastered forty of the words that are most frequently misspelled and eight words that are commonly confused and misused.

Check Your Reading POWER

It may **surprise** you to **discover** that a snake can swallow an animal that is two or three times larger than it is. The snake can do this because it is capable of **making** its jaws open extremely wide. It then grips its **victim** with needle-sharp teeth and gulps it down.

Snakes cannot move their eyelids. Their eyes are protected by thin, transparent coverings. Also, snakes do not have ears. However, snakes are not **dependent** upon ears for hearing. Snakes can **sense** sound by the vibrations of the ground. They are also very skilled, or proficient, at tracking other animals. A snake can **receive** and follow an animal's scent by **using** its tongue to pick up specks of dust. Snakes are **truly fascinating** creatures.

Put an X in the box next to the correct answer. After you have completed the exercise, check your answers.

Pick the Main Idea

1. This selection is mainly about
   - ☐ a. how snakes eat.
   - ☐ b. how snakes sense movement.
   - ☐ c. why snakes are fascinating.

Observe Supporting Details

2. Snakes do not have
   - ☐ a. bones.
   - ☐ b. ears.
   - ☐ c. tongues.

Watch for New Vocabulary

3. What is the meaning of the word proficient?
   - ☐ a. poor.
   - ☐ b. skilled.
   - ☐ c. difficult.

Explain Cause and Effect

4. A snake can tell that another creature is near by
   - ☐ a. sniffing its scent.
   - ☐ b. hearing its cries.
   - ☐ c. feeling the movement of the ground.

Read to Draw Inferences

5. This passage suggests that snakes
   - ☐ a. fear larger animals.
   - ☐ b. are helpless.
   - ☐ c. differ greatly from most animals.

More Spelling Power to You

Look closely at the ten boldface words in the passage. Write each word in a sentence and underline the spelling word. Study the words (see page 103). Then complete the spelling check on the next page. It contains all the words from this lesson.

Check Your Spelling Power

In each group of words, one word is misspelled. On the line, write the letter of the misspelled word.

1. ______	a. dependent	b. surprise	c. trully
2. ______	a. victim	b. makeing	c. sense
3. ______	a. descover	b. using	c. receive
4. ______	a. surprise	b. fasinating	c. dependent
5. ______	a. sence	b. truly	c. victim
6. ______	a. useing	b. dependent	c. receive
7. ______	a. making	b. discover	c. suprise
8. ______	a. sense	b. recieve	c. truly
9. ______	a. fascinating	b. victem	c. making
10. ______	a. using	b. surprise	c. dependant

Check your answers in the answer key on page 97. In your notebook, keep a list of the words you misspelled. Study those words until you master them.

Words Often Confused and Misused

Carefully study the meanings of the words and the sample sentences. Complete the exercise below by writing the words *accept* and *except* in the proper blanks.

accept The word *accept* is a verb. It means "to receive."

except The word *except* is usually a preposition that means "but."

With many thanks, I **accept** your electric potato peeler.
Everyone **except** Pat is singing off key.
I would **accept** the modesty award, **except** I don't deserve it.

1. I can ______________ anything ______________ criticism.

2. Everyone ______________ Henry was willing to ______________ my apology.

3. Please ______________ this pass, which is good any day of the week ______________ Friday.

Lesson 2

Check Your Reading POWER

The largest animal that has ever lived on our planet is still alive today. This enormous creature is the blue whale.

Found in oceans all over the world, the blue whale is **generally** twenty to thirty feet long at birth. It **usually** grows to about ninety feet, **although** some blue whales **approach** one hundred feet in length. A fully grown blue whale may **weigh** 350,000 pounds. That is about twice the <u>magnitude</u> of the **biggest** dinosaur on record.

Like all whales, the blue whale is a mammal. It is **equipped** with lungs and must **occasionally** surface for air. It can be **drowned** if it becomes trapped underwater without **sufficient** air.

Put an X in the box next to the correct answer. After you have completed the exercise, check your answers.

Pick the Main Idea

1. This selection is mainly about
   - ☐ a. where blue whales are found.
   - ☐ b. the biggest dinosaur on record.
   - ☐ c. the size of the blue whale.

Observe Supporting Details

2. The blue whale is a
   - ☐ a. fish.
   - ☐ b. reptile.
   - ☐ c. mammal.

Watch for New Vocabulary

3. What is the meaning of the word <u>magnitude</u>?
   - ☐ a. size
   - ☐ b. color
   - ☐ c. ability

Explain Cause and Effect

4. If a whale does not obtain air occasionally, it will
   - ☐ a. drown.
   - ☐ b. become trapped underwater.
   - ☐ c. use its lungs to produce air.

Read to Draw Inferences

5. This passage suggests that
   - ☐ a. most blue whales are one-hundred feet long.
   - ☐ b. a one-hundred-foot whale would be rare.
   - ☐ c. whales are weak for their size.

More Spelling Power to You

Look closely at the ten boldface words in the passage. Write each word in a sentence and underline the spelling word. Study the words (see page 103). Then complete the spelling check on the next page. It contains some words from the last lesson and most of the words from this lesson. Therefore, you must review all of the words you have learned before you complete the exercise. Concentrate on words that you previously misspelled.

Check Your Spelling Power

Circle the misspelled word in each of the following pairs of words. Then write the word correctly on the line provided.

__________ 1. receive
aproach

__________ 2. ocasionally
using

__________ 3. fascinating
drownd

__________ 4. bigest
dependent

__________ 5. trully
although

__________ 6. sense
wiegh

__________ 7. equipt
using

__________ 8. discover
usualy

__________ 9. sufficent
making

__________ 10. generally
suprise

Check your answers in the answer key on page 97. In your notebook, keep a list of the words you misspelled. Study those words until you master them.

Words Often Confused and Misused

Carefully study the meanings of the words and the sample sentences. Complete the exercise below by writing the words *loose* and *lose* in the proper blanks.

loose The word *loose* means "not tight" or "free." Note that *loose* rhymes with *noose.*

lose The word *lose* means "to misplace—not have any longer." Note that *lose* rhymes with *shoes.*

When the lion got **loose**, we went indoors.
I would rather **lose** my fortune than my good name.
If you **lose** ten pounds, your clothing will be **loose**.

1. A __________ thread can cause you to __________ a button.
2. If you continue to play with your __________ shoelaces, we may __________ the game.
3. After the tiger got __________, it managed to __________ its pursuers.

Now review the Words Often Confused and Misused from the last lesson. They will be included in the Cumulative Review following lesson 8.

Lesson 3

Check Your Reading POWER

Your sight **probably** is **all right** if you are "blind as a bat." That is because bats are not blind, though they may give that impression.

Scientists who have been **studying** bats have learned that bats employ a remarkable radarlike **system** that guides them at night. As the bat **flies** through the night sky, it repeatedly utters a short, high **shriek**. When the sound strikes an object, an echo bounces back. From the echo, the bat can tell the size and shape of the object. In that way, a bat can locate an insect in total darkness. The bat can then swoop **straight toward** it for food.

As the bat emits its high piercing sound, it turns its head from side to side. Perhaps the **awkward** twisting motion gives observers the idea that bats cannot see. However, the notion that bats are blind is **nonsense**.

Put an X in the box next to the correct answer. After you have completed the exercise, check your answers.

Pick the Main Idea

1. This passage is mainly about
   - ☐ a. how bats find their way at night.
   - ☐ b. ways in which scientists have been studying bats.
   - ☐ c. why bats cannot see well.

Observe Supporting Details

2. A bat twists its head from side to side when it
   - ☐ a. swoops toward an insect.
   - ☐ b. shrieks.
   - ☐ c. is attempting to hide.

Watch for New Vocabulary

3. What is the meaning of the word emits?
   - ☐ a. utters
   - ☐ b. catches
   - ☐ c. believes

Explain Cause and Effect

4. Bats use a kind of radar system to
   - ☐ a. help themselves fly.
   - ☐ b. locate and identify objects at night.
   - ☐ c. give the impression that they are blind.

Read to Draw Inferences

5. This passage suggests that bats
   - ☐ a. use their ears rather than their eyes to find their way at night.
   - ☐ b. have great difficulty in finding food in total darkness.
   - ☐ c. can see better than most animals.

More Spelling Power to You

Look closely at the ten boldface words in the passage. Write each word in a sentence and underline the spelling word. Study the words (see page 103). Then complete the spelling check on the next page. It contains some words from the last lesson and most of the words from this lesson. Therefore, you must review all of the words you have learned before you complete the exercise. Concentrate on words that you previously misspelled.

Check Your Spelling Power

Circle the misspelled word in each of the following groups of words. Then write the word correctly on the line provided.

______________	1. weigh	receive	shreik	sufficient
______________	2. approach	truly	alright	although
______________	3. akward	fascinating	using	equipped
______________	4. surprise	making	sense	nonsence
______________	5. probaly	drowned	victim	biggest
______________	6. discover	flys	dependent	all right
______________	7. studying	generaly	usually	occasionally
______________	8. toward	awkward	systim	truly
______________	9. straight	dependant	fascinating	all right
______________	10. makeing	using	surprise	receive

Check your answers in the answer key on page 97. In your notebook, keep a list of the words you misspelled. Study those words until you master them.

Words Often Confused and Misused

Carefully study the meanings of the words and the sample sentences. Complete the exercise below by writing the words *threw* and *through* in the proper blanks.

threw The word *threw* means "hurled." It is a verb—the past tense of *throw*.

through The word *through* is a preposition. It usually means "from end to end" or "into."

He **threw** a baseball with dazzling speed and remarkable control.
They rushed **through** the castle in search of an exit.
With a sudden twist, the horse **threw** its rider **through** the air.

1. To no one's surprise, Marie ______________ the basketball right ______________ the hoop.
2. Sam ______________ his scarf around his neck and marched fearlessly ______________ the crowd.
3. We carefully looked ______________ the book Omara ______________ at us.

Now review the Words Often Confused and Misused from previous lessons. They will be included in the Cumulative Review following lesson 8.

Check Your Reading POWER

You may find it hard to stomach these facts about animals.

The crocodile, **believe** it or not, carries several pounds of small stones in its stomach. There is a simple **explanation** for this **unusual** fact. It is **impossible** for the crocodile to chew its food; it must swallow it whole. The stones, **therefore,** are indispensable, or **absolutely necessary.** They help the crocodile grind up the food so that it can be digested.

Speaking of stomachs, the next time you have a **terrible ache** in your stomach, be thankful that you're not a hippopotamus, because then you'd really be in pain. A hippo's stomach is ten feet long. Be **grateful,** too, that you're not a cow, for cows have four stomachs.

Put an X in the box next to the correct answer. After you have completed the exercise, check your answers.

Pick the Main Idea

1. This selection is mainly about
   - ☐ a. the eating habits of the crocodile.
   - ☐ b. the number of stomach aches in animals.
   - ☐ c. the fact that animals have many different kinds of stomachs.

Observe Supporting Details

2. How many stomachs do cows have?
   - ☐ a. four
   - ☐ b. ten
   - ☐ c. six

Watch for New Vocabulary

3. In the passage, indispensable means
   - ☐ a. absolutely necessary.
   - ☐ b. sometimes helpful.
   - ☐ c. not needed.

Explain Cause and Effect

4. A crocodile uses the stones in its stomach to help it
   - ☐ a. swallow its food.
   - ☐ b. chew its food.
   - ☐ c. grind up its food.

Read to Draw Inferences

5. This passage suggests that
   - ☐ a. crocodiles are born with stones in their stomachs.
   - ☐ b. human beings have better stomachs than other animals do.
   - ☐ c. animals' stomachs do not all work the same way.

More Spelling Power to You

Look closely at the ten boldface words in the passage. Write each word in a sentence and underline the spelling word. Study the words (see page 103). Then complete the spelling check on the next page. It contains some words from the last lesson and most of the words from this lesson. Therefore, you must review all of the words you have learned before you complete the exercise. Concentrate on words that you previously misspelled.

Check Your Spelling Power

Underline the misspelled word in each sentence. Then write the word correctly on the line provided.

______________ 1. It is impossable to receive high marks without studying.

______________ 2. There is probably a simple explaination for that unusual occurrence.

______________ 3. The movie had a facinating plot, although the acting was terrible.

______________ 4. I am truly gratefull to you for showing such good sense.

______________ 5. Even though her ankle began to acke, Louise kept running straight toward the finish line.

______________ 6. The spacecraft is dipendent upon the landing system it is carrying.

______________ 7. The beast is occasionally dangerous; therfore you must approach it with care.

______________ 8. It was absolutly the biggest surprise of her life.

______________ 9. They beleive the victim drowned long before he was found by the rescue workers.

______________ 10. On a biking trip, it is neccesary to be equipped with supplies that are lightweight.

Check your answers in the answer key on page 97. In your notebook, keep a list of the words you misspelled. Study those words until you master them.

Words Often Confused and Misused

Carefully study the meanings of the words and the sample sentences. Complete the exercise below by writing the words *quiet* and *quite* in the proper blanks.

quiet The word *quiet* means "not loud" or "calm."

quite The word *quite* means "very" or "completely."

A piercing scream shattered the quiet of the night.
The coach was quite satisfied with her team's play.
A leopard, gliding with quiet grace, is quite a moving sight.

1. Although Tino is very __________, he is __________ popular.
2. I was __________ amazed that you remained __________ for so long.
3. On the wall hung a __________ beautiful painting of a __________ country scene.

Now review the Words Often Confused and Misused from previous lessons. They will be included in the Cumulative Review following lesson 8.

Unit 2

People and Animals

When you have completed this unit, you will have mastered eighty of the words that are most frequently misspelled and sixteen words that are commonly confused and misused.

Check Your Reading POWER

Dian Fossey was an American scientist who studied animals, especially wild gorillas. Fossey made many trips to Africa, **beginning** in 1963 **until** her death in 1985. In Africa, she managed to **succeed** in observing numerous mountain gorillas. Fossey was able to **acquire** a great deal of information about their habits. She learned that although they are huge animals, gorillas are gentle and friendly. Fossey's <u>illustrious</u> **career** was suddenly cut short when she was found murdered at her jungle camp. It was never determined who was **responsible** for her death.

The next time you are in a **library,** look for the book *Gorillas in the Mist*. This book, which was **written** in 1983, offers an **interesting** and vivid **description** of the lives of mountain gorillas.

Put an X in the box next to the correct answer. After you have completed the exercise, check your answers.

Pick the Main Idea

1. This selection is mainly about
   - ☐ a. an interesting book.
   - ☐ b. kinds of wild animals.
   - ☐ c. Dian Fossey, an American scientist.

Observe Supporting Details

2. *Gorillas in the Mist* was written in
   - ☐ a. 1963.
   - ☐ b. 1983.
   - ☐ c. 1985.

Watch for New Vocabulary

3. What is the meaning of the word <u>illustrious</u>?
   - ☐ a. dull
   - ☐ b. poor
   - ☐ c. famous

Explain Cause and Effect

4. Fossey traveled to Africa often because she
   - ☐ a. was a person who just couldn't settle down.
   - ☐ b. had no real home.
   - ☐ c. was interested in studying mountain gorillas.

Read to Draw Inferences

5. We may infer that Fossey
   - ☐ a. knew very little about wild animals.
   - ☐ b. usually killed the animals she studied.
   - ☐ c. sometimes lived in difficult and dangerous conditions.

More Spelling Power to You

Look closely at the ten boldface words in the passage. Write each word in a sentence and underline the spelling word. Study the words (see page 103). Then complete the spelling check on the next page. It contains some words from the last lesson and most of the words from this lesson. Therefore, you must review all of the words you have learned before you complete the exercise. Concentrate on words that you previously misspelled.

Check Your Spelling Power

In each group of words, one word is misspelled. On the line, write the letter of the misspelled word.

1. ________	a. truly	b. responsable	c. receive
2. ________	a. career	b. therefore	c. necesary
3. ________	a. libary	b. sense	c. ache
4. ________	a. grateful	b. intresting	c. although
5. ________	a. begining	b. weigh	c. impossible
6. ________	a. written	b. shreik	c. studying
7. ________	a. occasionally	b. nonsense	c. untill
8. ________	a. suceed	b. fascinating	c. flies
9. ________	a. absolutely	b. discription	c. surprise
10. ________	a. discover	b. dependent	c. aquire

Check your answers in the answer key on page 97. In your notebook, keep a list of the words you misspelled. Study those words until you master them.

Words Often Confused and Misused

Carefully study the meanings of the words and the sample sentences. Complete the exercise below by writing the words *it's* and *its* in the proper blanks.

its The word *its* is a possessive pronoun. It shows possession or ownership. *Its* means "belonging to it."

it's The word *it's* is a contraction (shortened form) of *it is.* The apostrophe takes the place of the letter *i* in *is. It's* always means "it is."

The dog lowered **its** head, sniffed **its** bowl, and wagged **its** tail.
Dave says **it's** a good movie, but Beth says **it's** boring.
I think **it's** amazing how a cat always manages to land on **its** paws.

1. Of course, ________ dangerous to be in a car that has lost ________ steering.
2. Remember, ________ not winning or losing that counts; ________ the way you play the game.
3. When a crowd rises to ________ feet and shouts "Bravo," that means ________ delighted with the performance.

Now review the Words Often Confused and Misused from previous lessons. They will be included in the Cumulative Review following lesson 8.

Lesson 6

Check Your Reading POWER

Two brothers named Montgolfier launched the first air travelers.

It all started in 1782, when the Montgolfiers were **busy** working in their shop. They **accidentally** made a discovery that filled them with **excitement.** They learned that hot air has the power to make things rise.

It soon became the brothers' **ambition** to construct a **balloon** that could carry passengers into the air. The Montgolfiers conducted many experiments. They were **eventually** ready for the crucial test.

It **happened** in June 1783. The Montgolfiers filled a large balloon with hot air and set it free. It would be difficult to **describe** the brothers' joy and **relief** as they watched the balloon soar to a **height** of six thousand feet. Aboard were the first air travelers—a chicken, a duck, and a sheep.

Put an X in the box next to the correct answer. After you have completed the exercise, check your answers.

Pick the Main Idea

1. This selection is mainly about how
   - ☐ a. the Montgolfiers made an amazing discovery.
   - ☐ b. a balloon rose to a height of six thousand feet.
   - ☐ c. three animals became the first air travelers.

Observe Supporting Details

2. The Montgolfiers' successful balloon flight took place in
   - ☐ a. 1782.
   - ☐ b. 1783.
   - ☐ c. 1784.

Watch for New Vocabulary

3. What is the meaning of the word crucial as it is used in the passage?
   - ☐ a. first
   - ☐ b. most dangerous
   - ☐ c. most important

Explain Cause and Effect

4. When they discovered that hot air could make things rise, the Montgolfiers
   - ☐ a. were filled with relief.
   - ☐ b. decided to build a balloon.
   - ☐ c. became the first air travelers.

Read to Draw Inferences

5. The Montgolfiers probably selected animals to be the balloon's first passengers because
   - ☐ a. the Montgolfiers loved animals.
   - ☐ b. animals are lighter than people.
   - ☐ c. the Montgolfiers thought it was too dangerous to send a human being.

More Spelling Power to You

Look closely at the ten boldface words in the passage. Write each word in a sentence and underline the spelling word. Study the words (see page 103). Then complete the spelling check on the next page. It contains some words from the last lesson and most of the words from this lesson. Therefore, you must review all of the words you have learned before you complete the exercise. Concentrate on words that you previously misspelled.

Check Your Spelling Power

Circle the misspelled word in each of the following pairs of words. Then write the word correctly on the line provided.

______________ 1. succeed
discribe

______________ 2. writen
busy

______________ 3. until
baloon

______________ 4. recieve
happened

______________ 5. accidentaly
straight

______________ 6. beginning
releif

______________ 7. responsible
excitment

______________ 8. height
usualy

______________ 9. eventualy
interesting

______________ 10. alright
ambition

Check your answers in the answer key on page 97. In your notebook, keep a list of the words you misspelled. Study those words until you master them.

Words Often Confused and Misused

Carefully study the meanings of the words and the sample sentences. Complete the exercise below by writing the words *weather* and *whether* in the proper blanks.

weather The word *weather* refers to the climate or the condition of the air.

whether The word *whether* is a conjunction that often means "if."

I listen to the weather report every day.
Mrs. Lee asked Hector whether he wanted to join the Science Club.
We are going on vacation whether the weather is good or bad.

1. Amy didn't know ______________ to take an umbrella, because the ______________ report said there was a slight chance of rain.
2. Although Mr. Cooper enjoys the ______________ in Maine, he can't decide ______________ to accept a job there or not.
3. According to the umpire, ______________ or not the game will be played depends upon the ______________.

Now review the Words Often Confused and Misused from previous lessons. They will be included in the Cumulative Review following lesson 8.

Lesson 7

Check Your Reading POWER

It was a long and difficult journey—1,135 miles through two mountain ranges and **across** the Yukon River. But when it was completed, Libby Riddle had reason to **celebrate.** She had won Alaska's Thirteenth Annual Anchorage-to-Nome Dogsled Race.

The most trying part of the three-week race was the struggle **against** abominable weather. Snow kept **coming** down **continually,** and a blizzard made it hard to see. But Libby managed to **conquer** the elements and keep moving **forward.**

According to the winner, most of the credit for her victory should go to the fifteen **courageous** dogs that pulled the sled. In **preparation** for the journey, Libby selected the healthiest and best dogs she could find to **accompany** her. Now she wishes she could share the $50,000 first prize with them.

Put an X in the box next to the correct answer. After you have completed the exercise, check your answers.

Pick the Main Idea

1. This selection is mainly about
   - ☐ a. the distance from Anchorage to Nome.
   - ☐ b. how to conquer the elements.
   - ☐ c. a dogsled race in Alaska.

Observe Supporting Details

2. How long did the trip take?
   - ☐ a. two weeks
   - ☐ b. three weeks
   - ☐ c. fifteen weeks

Watch for New Vocabulary

3. What is the meaning of the word abominable?
   - ☐ a. very unpleasant or miserable
   - ☐ b. enjoyable or delightful
   - ☐ c. having to do with the abdomen or stomach

Explain Cause and Effect

4. In part, Libby Riddle's victory was due to the
   - ☐ a. efforts of her courageous dogs.
   - ☐ b. unusually fine weather.
   - ☐ c. fact that the journey was long and difficult.

Read to Draw Inferences

5. This passage suggests that Libby Riddle
   - ☐ a. won the race through sheer luck.
   - ☐ b. did not prepare well for the race.
   - ☐ c. had both strength and determination.

More Spelling Power to You

Look closely at the ten boldface words in the passage. Write each word in a sentence and underline the spelling word. Study the words (see page 103). Then complete the spelling check on the next page. It contains some words from the last lesson and most of the words from this lesson. Therefore, you must review all of the words you have learned before you complete the exercise. Concentrate on words that you previously misspelled.

Check Your Spelling Power

Circle the misspelled word in each of the following groups of words. Then write the word correctly on the line provided.

______________	1.	accidentally	eventually	continualy	generally
______________	2.	accross	equipped	approach	necessary
______________	3.	making	coming	useing	biggest
______________	4.	conquor	discover	therefore	awkward
______________	5.	ache	straight	dependent	foward
______________	6.	absolutely	couragous	interesting	grateful
______________	7.	celabrate	believe	impossible	terrible
______________	8.	describe	discover	preperation	busy
______________	9.	acompany	balloon	truly	written
______________	10.	acquire	career	against	ocasionally

Check your answers in the answer key on page 97. In your notebook, keep a list of the words you misspelled. Study those words until you master them.

Words Often Confused and Misused

Carefully study the meanings of the words and the sample sentences. Complete the exercise below by writing *all ready* and *already* in the proper blanks.

all ready The words *all ready* mean "all prepared" or "all set."

already The word *already* means "previously" or "earlier."

The musicians were **all ready** to play.
Raymond has **already** seen that play three times.
We were **all ready** to go to the airport, when we learned that the plane had **already** arrived.

1. Although we have ______________ played their team twice, we are ______________ to play them again.
2. The buses are ______________ to leave; in fact one bus has ______________ left.
3. The police have ______________ been called, and they are ______________ to make the arrest.

Now review the Words Often Confused and Misused from previous lessons. They will be included in the Cumulative Review following lesson 8.

Lesson 8

Check Your Reading POWER

When Miami's MetroZoo started **losing** money, someone thought of a **brilliant** and amusing way to increase **attendance.**

Visitors to the zoo were treated to an added attraction: a new specimen that wore a dark **business** suit, a white shirt, and a tie. It roamed around its pen and did many **familiar** things. For example, it brushed its teeth, shaved its face, listened to the radio, watched television, and read a newspaper. On **occasion,** it ate a meal that was offered by its keeper. Although the creature refused to **speak** to the patrons that regularly gathered around its pen, it willingly shook hands with them.

This **extraordinary exhibit** is one that you are likely to **recognize.** It is called "Urban Man."

Put an X in the box next to the correct answer. After you have completed the exercise, check your answers.

Pick the Main Idea

1. This selection is mainly about
   - ☐ a. visitors to the Miami MetroZoo.
   - ☐ b. an unusual exhibit at a zoo.
   - ☐ c. why a zoo was losing money.

Observe Supporting Details

2. The specimen refused to
   - ☐ a. shake hands with visitors.
   - ☐ b. talk to zoo visitors.
   - ☐ c. read a newspaper.

Watch for New Vocabulary

3. As used in this selection, the word patrons means
   - ☐ a. paying visitors.
   - ☐ b. friends or neighbors.
   - ☐ c. specimens or examples.

Explain Cause and Effect

4. The new specimen was added to the zoo in order to
   - ☐ a. increase attendance.
   - ☐ b. show people what "Urban Man" looks like.
   - ☐ c. hand out information about the zoo.

Read to Draw Inferences

5. The new exhibit probably resulted in
   - ☐ a. anger rather than amusement on the part of most visitors.
   - ☐ b. decreased attendance at the zoo.
   - ☐ c. increased publicity about the zoo.

More Spelling Power to You

Look closely at the ten boldface words in the passage. Write each word in a sentence and underline the spelling word. Study the words (see page 103). Then complete the spelling check on the next page. It contains some words from the last lesson and most of the words from this lesson. Therefore, you must review all of the words you have learned before you complete the exercise. Concentrate on words that you previously misspelled.

Check Your Spelling Power

Underline the misspelled word in each sentence. Then write the word correctly on the line provided.

_______________ 1. He had perfect attendence from the beginning of the year until now.

_______________ 2. It was a brilliant plan, although it failed to suceed.

_______________ 3. I could hardly describe my excitement and relief at finally hearing a familar voice.

_______________ 4. Look in the library for *The Call of the Wild*, the extraordnary tale of a courageous dog.

_______________ 5. Gene has grown so much in height that it's almost impossible to reconize him.

_______________ 6. I am never too busy to celebrate a truly happy ocassion.

_______________ 7. The *Titanic* eventually sank, after the ship accidentally smashed into an iceberg and began loseing its power.

_______________ 8. In preparation for his new career, Sal planned to acquire some busness skills.

_______________ 9. The director said, "It is necessary for you to speek much louder if you want to be absolutely certain of being heard."

_______________ 10. The jury bent forward to see exibit A—a letter written by the victim.

Check your answers in the answer key on page 97. In your notebook, keep a list of the words you misspelled. Study those words until you master them.

Words Often Confused and Misused

Carefully study the meanings of the words and the sample sentences. Complete the exercise below by writing the words *whose* and *who's* in the proper blanks.

whose The word *whose* is a possessive adjective or pronoun meaning "of whom" or "of which."

who's The word *who's* is a contraction. It means "who is" or "who has." The apostrophe takes the place of the missing letter or letters.

I wonder whose book this is.
That's Chandra, who's the best chess player in school.
Whose house is the party at, and who's going to be there?

1. I don't know __________ idea it was or __________ to blame.

2. Louisa, __________ painting won first prize, is the girl __________ standing near the door.

3. Anyone __________ played soccer before should talk to Mr. Larsen, __________ team needs players.

Now review the Words Often Confused and Misused from lessons 1–8. They will be included in the Cumulative Review that begins on the next page.

Cumulative Review of Units 1 and 2

A. In each of the following groups of words, one word is misspelled. Circle the misspelled word. Then write the word correctly on the line to the left.

________________ 1. alright
busy
happened

________________ 2. although
probably
equipt

________________ 3. sufficient
eventualy
ache

________________ 4. responsible
recognize
foward

________________ 5. against
drownd
celebrate

________________ 6. aproach
exhibit
beginning

________________ 7. bussiness
describe
system

________________ 8. therefore
generaly
continually

________________ 9. acidentally
accompany
making

________________ 10. sense
awkward
nonsence

B. Fill in the blanks in the words to create words that are spelled correctly. Then write the words on the lines to the left.

________________ 11. terr __ ble

________________ 12. d __ scover

________________ 13. attend __ nce

________________ 14. prep __ ration

________________ 15. conqu __ r

________________ 16. spe __ k

________________ 17. imposs __ ble

________________ 18. r __ sponsible

________________ 19. d __ pend __ nt

________________ 20. d __ scr __ ption

C. The letters *ie* or *ei* are missing from each of the words below. Fill in the blanks in each word to spell the word correctly. Then write the word on the line to the left.

________________ 21. rec __ __ ve

________________ 22. h __ __ ght

________________ 23. rel __ __ f

________________ 24. shr __ __ k

________________ 25. bel __ __ ve

D. In each of the following sentences, one of the three underlined words is misspelled. Circle the misspelled word. Then write the word correctly on the line before the sentence.

________________ 26. Our libary is usually open until nine o'clock on Thursday.

________________ 27. We are certain you will succeed in your fasinating new career.

_______________ 28. There was excitment in the air as the balloon slowly started coming down.

_______________ 29. The *Diary of a Young Girl* is one of the most interisting and extraordinary books ever written.

_______________ 30. Everyone agreed it was truly a thoughtful and unusual suprise.

_______________ 31. It is Chantel's ambition to aquire the biggest collection of baseball cards in the world.

_______________ 32. Is that Paul skating straiht across the rink toward us?

_______________ 33. It is absolutely neccessary for me to spend more time studying.

_______________ 34. Are you familiar with the explanation of how an airplane flys?

_______________ 35. On this occassion, let us show you how grateful we are to you for your courageous deed.

E. Each of the following sentences contains two words in parentheses. Underline the one that makes the sentence correct. Then write the word on the line to the left.

_______________ 36. Only the *drip, drip, drip* of a faucet broke the (quiet, quite).

_______________ 37. Good (weather, whether) always seems to lift everyone's spirits.

_______________ 38. Time flies—we're (all ready, already) doing this cumulative review.

_______________ 39. The injured bird kept trying to flap (its, it's) wing.

_______________ 40. Finally the sun broke (threw, through) the clouds.

_______________ 41. Can you tell me (whose, who's) in charge here?

_______________ 42. Since it is raining, I'll gladly (accept, except) your offer of a ride home.

_______________ 43. Did anyone (loose, lose) a quarter with George Washington's face on it?

_______________ 44. The room became (quiet, quite) cold after the furnace broke down.

_______________ 45. The juggler (threw, through) one orange after another into the air.

_______________ 46. I wonder if (its, it's) true that an elephant never forgets.

_______________ 47. No matter how many times he was tied up, the great Houdini always managed to get (loose, lose).

_______________ 48. Sacha loves every season (accept, except) winter.

_______________ 49. José is the student (whose, who's) poetry has won awards.

_______________ 50. We couldn't decide (weather, whether) the glass was half empty or half full.

Unit 3

Food for Thought

When you have completed this unit, you will have mastered 120 of the words that are most frequently misspelled and 25 words that are commonly confused and misused.

Lesson 9

Check Your Reading POWER

Do you appreciate salt? Chances are you see and use it so **often** that you take it for granted. But there are more than ten thousand uses for salt, and it has **always** held a place of **importance** in daily life.

At one time salt was so **valuable** and rare that it was used as money. In fact, the word *salary* comes from the word *salt*. During early Roman times, each **soldier** in Julius Caesar's army was **paid** a portion of his earnings in salt. That **quantity** was known as his *salarium*—or **salary.**

The phrase "not worth his salt" has a **similar** derivation, or origin. It is an expression of **criticism.** Someone who is "not worth his salt" is not worth his pay.

Put an X in the box next to the correct answer. After you have completed the exercise, check your answers.

Pick the Main Idea

1. This selection is mainly about
   - ☐ a. the ten thousand uses of salt.
   - ☐ b. Julius Caesar's army.
   - ☐ c. the derivation of the word salary.

Observe Supporting Details

2. Through the years, salt has
   - ☐ a. had little value.
   - ☐ b. always been important.
   - ☐ c. always been easy to obtain.

Watch for New Vocabulary

3. What is the meaning of the word derivation?
   - ☐ a. goal
   - ☐ b. meaning
   - ☐ c. origin

Explain Cause and Effect

4. Salt was once used as money because it was
   - ☐ a. rare and valuable.
   - ☐ b. easy to count.
   - ☐ c. very tasty.

Read to Draw Inferences

5. Someone who is "worth her salt" is probably
   - ☐ a. lazy.
   - ☐ b. a good worker.
   - ☐ c. being paid too much.

More Spelling Power to You

Look closely at the ten boldface words in the passage. Write each word in a sentence and underline the spelling word. Study the words (see page 103). Then complete the spelling check on the next page. It contains some words from the last lesson and most of the words from this lesson. Therefore, you must review all of the words you have learned before you complete the exercise. Concentrate on words that you previously misspelled.

Check Your Spelling Power

In each group of words, one word is misspelled. On the line, write the letter of the misspelled word.

	a.	b.	c.
1. ________	a. occasionally	b. truly	c. ofen
2. ________	a. similar	b. although	c. flys
3. ________	a. responsible	b. salery	c. beginning
4. ________	a. payed	b. receive	c. describe
5. ________	a. interesting	b. explenation	c. valuable
6. ________	a. balloon	b. weigh	c. criticicm
7. ________	a. quantity	b. straigt	c. until
8. ________	a. agenst	b. always	c. acquire
9. ________	a. importence	b. written	c. therefore
10. ________	a. accompany	b. ambishion	c. soldier

Check your answers in the answer key on page 98. In your notebook, keep a list of the words you misspelled. Study those words until you master them.

Words Often Confused and Misused

Carefully study the meanings of the words and the sample sentences. Complete the exercise below by writing *to, too,* and *two* in the proper blanks.

to The word *to* is usually a preposition that means "in the direction of." Sometimes *to* is used as part of a verb, as in *to speak*.

too The word *too* means "very," "also," or "more than enough."

two The word *two* refers to the number 2.

Linda is planning to go to the department store to buy a notebook to take to school.
Someone once said that we grow old too soon and wise too late; I believe that, too.
The two front tires need two pounds of air.
After Yoshi ate two sandwiches, he was too full to move.

1. If you go ________ the supermarket, ________, please purchase ________ grapefruits and some apples.
2. In order ________ get ________ my uncle's house, you must take ________ buses, and a subway ________.
3. Do you think it is ________ late for us ________ hurry ________ the box office ________ buy ________ tickets?

Now review the Words Often Confused and Misused from previous lessons. They will be included in the Cumulative Review following lesson 16.

Check Your Reading POWER

Every day, more than **forty million** Americans enjoy a hamburger or a **sandwich.** Surprisingly, perhaps, these popular "American" foods originated in other countries.

You may have **guessed** that the **source** of the hamburger's name was the city of Hamburg, in Germany. Actually, however, the hamburger originated in Russia, where it was eaten raw. German sailors later took the recipe back to Hamburg. The natives there, however, found eating raw meat **disagreeable.** They decided to broil it. The result was the hamburger.

As for the sandwich, England's fourth Earl of Sandwich was playing cards when he began to get hungry. The earl was reluctant to **interrupt** his game, yet was **anxious** to eat. He solved his <u>dilemma</u> by instructing a servant to bring him a piece of roast beef between two slices of bread. That **permitted** the earl to eat with one hand and play cards with the other. And so the sandwich, which still bears the earl's name, came into **existence.**

Put an X in the box next to the correct answer. After you have completed the exercise, check your answers.

Pick the Main Idea

1. This selection is mainly about
   - ☐ a. how German sailors brought a recipe to Hamburg.
   - ☐ b. England's fourth Earl of Sandwich.
   - ☐ c. how the hamburger and the sandwich originated.

Observe Supporting Details

2. Raw hamburgers were first eaten in
   - ☐ a. Germany.
   - ☐ b. Russia.
   - ☐ c. England.

Watch for New Vocabulary

3. What is the meaning of the word <u>dilemma</u>?
   - ☐ a. problem
   - ☐ b. anxiety
   - ☐ c. hunger

Explain Cause and Effect

4. The sandwich was invented as a result of
   - ☐ a. the imagination of a clever servant.
   - ☐ b. an earl's desire both to eat and to play cards.
   - ☐ c. a very interesting card game.

Read to Draw Inferences

5. This passage suggests that foods
   - ☐ a. usually come into being for odd reasons.
   - ☐ b. are sometimes named for their origins.
   - ☐ c. travel quickly from one place to another.

More Spelling Power to You

Look closely at the ten boldface words in the passage. Write each word in a sentence and underline the spelling word. Study the words (see page 103). Then complete the spelling check on the next page. It contains some words from the last lesson and most of the words from this lesson. Therefore, you must review all of the words you have learned before you complete the exercise. Concentrate on words that you previously misspelled.

Check Your Spelling Power

Circle the misspelled word in each of the following pairs of words. Then write the word correctly on the line provided.

________________	**1.**	sandwich	allways
________________	**2.**	fourty	exhibit
________________	**3.**	akward	guessed
________________	**4.**	million	succed
________________	**5.**	source	extrordinary
________________	**6.**	existance	conquer
________________	**7.**	library	interupt
________________	**8.**	permited	business
________________	**9.**	anxious	valuble
________________	**10.**	courageous	disagreable

Check your answers in the answer key on page 98. In your notebook, keep a list of the words you misspelled. Study those words until you master them.

Words Often Confused and Misused

Carefully study the meanings of the words and the sample sentences. Complete the exercise below by writing *than* and *then* in the proper blanks.

than The word *than* is a conjunction or a preposition used in comparisons.

then The word *then* is usually an adverb or a noun that means "at that time."

Mount McKinley is higher **than** Mount Logan, but Mount Everest is higher **than** Mount McKinley.
The meeting is at four o'clock; I'll see you **then.**
Then Mr. Garcia asked whether Ken was taller **than** his brother.

1. I like fall better __________ spring because Thanksgiving comes __________.
2. Su-Mei hurt her ankle when she stumbled; __________ she began running more slowly __________ usual.
3. When my grandfather talks about "the good old days," he says that prices __________ were much lower __________ they are today.

Now review the Words Often Confused and Misused from previous lessons. They will be included in the Cumulative Review following lesson 16.

Check Your Reading POWER

Because of the expression "as American as apple pie," you might **naturally** **suppose** that apple pie is native to the United States. Like the hamburger and the sandwich, however, apple pie was invented in a foreign land. The French brought it to North America centuries ago.

Pies of all kinds have been popular in Europe for more than a thousand years. The ancient Romans, for example, loved to eat pies filled with meat, fish, or fowl. Strange as it sounds, a pie made with live birds was a special **banquet** dish.

The expression "as American as apple pie" probably developed because of the **genuine** ardor exhibited for apple pie **among** people of the United States. Surveys show that they **prefer** it by far to any other dessert. So the next time you order apple pie in a **restaurant** or **cafeteria,** be aware that you are **having** many Americans' **favorite** dessert.

Put an X in the box next to the correct answer. After you have completed the exercise, check your answers.

Pick the Main Idea

1. This selection is mainly about
   - ☐ a. how the French brought apple pie to North America.
   - ☐ b. the history of pie.
   - ☐ c. apple pie as the favorite dessert in the United States.

Observe Supporting Details

2. Pies made of live birds were once served by
   - ☐ a. ancient Romans.
   - ☐ b. early Americans.
   - ☐ c. the French, centuries ago.

Watch for New Vocabulary

3. From the context of the paragraph in which the word appears, you can tell that ardor means
   - ☐ a. patriotism.
   - ☐ b. belief.
   - ☐ c. enthusiasm.

Explain Cause and Effect

4. It is likely that the expression "as American as apple pie" came about due to the
   - ☐ a. fact that apple pie is native to the United States.
   - ☐ b. popularity of apple pie in the United States.
   - ☐ c. result of a survey of Americans.

Read to Draw Inferences

5. This passage suggests that pies are
   - ☐ a. an old food rather than a new one.
   - ☐ b. not enjoyed very much in Europe.
   - ☐ c. the most popular type of dessert the world over.

More Spelling Power to You

Look closely at the ten boldface words in the passage. Write each word in a sentence and underline the spelling word. Study the words (see page 103). Then complete the spelling check on the next page. It contains some words from the last lesson and most of the words from this lesson. Therefore, you must review all of the words you have learned before you complete the exercise. Concentrate on words that you previously misspelled.

Check Your Spelling Power

Circle the misspelled word in each of the following groups of words. Then write the word correctly on the line provided.

________	1. importance	cafateria	often	using
________	2. haveing	usually	forty	victim
________	3. among	biggest	dependent	similiar
________	4. paid	shriek	sandwitch	probably
________	5. necessary	preferr	grateful	genuine
________	6. interrupt	system	written	naturaly
________	7. suppose	milion	existence	impossible
________	8. disagreeable	excitement	restarant	brilliant
________	9. weight	career	favrite	description
________	10. banquit	accidentally	permitted	recognize

Check your answers in the answer key on page 98. In your notebook, keep a list of the words you misspelled. Study those words until you master them.

Words Often Confused and Misused

Carefully study the meanings of the words and the sample sentences. Complete the exercise below by writing *weak* and *week* in the proper blanks.

weak — The word *weak* means "feeble or lacking strength."

week — The word *week* means "seven days, one after another."

The old horse seemed too weak to pull the carriage.
Let's make plans to go to the museum next week or the following week.
The week after she had the flu, Liz still felt tired and weak.

1. Although Simon is sometimes a ________ batter, he certainly hit the ball well last ________.
2. At the beginning of the ________, Fernando's composition was poorly organized and ________; by the end of the ________, it was outstanding.
3. The doctor said, "If you still feel ________ in a ________, make an appointment to see me."

Now review the Words Often Confused and Misused from previous lessons. They will be included in the Cumulative Review following lesson 16.

Check Your Reading POWER

What makes popcorn pop? Unlike **ordinary** corn, popcorn is composed of **extremely** hard kernels that have waterproof shells. As a kernel is heated, the moisture inside it turns to steam. When the **temperature** rises **enough,** the steam explodes the kernel, causing a *pop!* to **occur.**

Popping popcorn is fun, but few people realize or **appreciate** how long popcorn has been **around.** Long **before** Columbus began his explorations, the **Indian** people of the Americas knew about popcorn. Unpopped kernels that are more than a thousand years old have been discovered, still intact, in Peru. And popped corn more than five thousand years old has been found **buried** in a cave in New Mexico.

Put an X in the box next to the correct answer. After you have completed the exercise, check your answers.

Pick the Main Idea

1. This selection is mainly about
   - ☐ a. the Indian people of the Americas.
   - ☐ b. the history of corn.
   - ☐ c. how long popcorn has been around.

Observe Supporting Details

2. Which of the following is true of popcorn kernels?
   - ☐ a. They are extremely soft.
   - ☐ b. They never explode.
   - ☐ c. They have waterproof shells.

Watch for New Vocabulary

3. What is the meaning of the word intact?
   - ☐ a. undamaged
   - ☐ b. broken
   - ☐ c. thoughtful

Explain Cause and Effect

4. What causes popcorn to pop?
   - ☐ a. steam
   - ☐ b. cold water
   - ☐ c. air pressure

Read to Draw Inferences

5. This passage suggests that popcorn
   - ☐ a. is purely an American treat.
   - ☐ b. was first grown in the Americas.
   - ☐ c. was eaten by Columbus on his voyage to America.

More Spelling Power to You

Look closely at the ten boldface words in the passage. Write each word in a sentence and underline the spelling word. Study the words (see page 103). Then complete the spelling check on the next page. It contains some words from the last lesson and most of the words from this lesson. Therefore, you must review all of the words you have learned before you complete the exercise. Concentrate on words that you previously misspelled.

Check Your Spelling Power

Underline the misspelled word in each sentence. Then write the word correctly on the line provided.

______________ 1. If you try hard enough, you will eventuelly succeed.

______________ 2. I apreciate winning, but on occasion one can learn a lesson by losing.

______________ 3. Leon did not feel all right; he had a temperture and a headache.

______________ 4. I'm anxious to visit Acoma, where my favorite indian pottery is made.

______________ 5. The frightened rabbit looked around, saw nothing, and hurried with releif straight toward its burrow.

______________ 6. They planned an extremly large banquet to celebrate the occasion.

______________ 7. Monday started as an ordinery day, but what happened later was truly amazing.

______________ 8. A meteor, whose source was more than forty million miles away, fell to the earth and was buryed in the ground.

______________ 9. Plan to arrive an hour befor the gates open, since attendance is expected to be high.

______________ 10. When you feel strong enough to speak, describe what did ocurr.

Check your answers in the answer key on page 98. In your notebook, keep a list of the words you misspelled. Study those words until you master them.

Words Often Confused and Misused

Carefully study the meanings of the words and the sample sentences. Complete the exercise below by writing *your* and *you're* in the proper blanks.

your The word *your* is a possessive pronoun meaning "belonging to you."

you're The word *you're* is a contraction meaning "you are." The apostrophe takes the place of the letter *a* in *are.*

Please introduce me to **your** brother and **your** sister, and say that I'm **your** favorite teacher.
When **you're** right **you're** right, but when **you're** wrong **you're** wrong.
Your report card shows that **you're** improving greatly.

1. Although __________ the last person in line, __________ turn will come before __________ aware of it.

2. Perhaps you should make art __________ career, because __________ paintings demonstrate that __________ very talented.

3. Now that __________ doing so well, speak to __________ employer about __________ chances of getting a raise.

Now review the Words Often Confused and Misused from previous lessons. They will be included in the Cumulative Review following lesson 16.

Unit 4

Presenting the Presidents

When you have completed this unit, you will have mastered 160 of the words that are most frequently misspelled and 33 words that are commonly confused and misused.

Lesson 13

Check Your Reading POWER

For seven years, President Theodore Roosevelt lived with a bullet in his chest. This strange story began in October 1912, when a man named John F. Schrank made an assassination **attempt** on the president. Schrank shot Roosevelt half an hour before the **chief** executive was about to make a **speech** in Milwaukee. The bullet, **fortunately,** struck a metal eyeglass case in Roosevelt's pocket and was diverted from his heart.

Roosevelt placed a **handkerchief** over the wound and ordered his aides to **proceed** to the auditorium. There he delivered his talk on **schedule.** Doctors later determined that it was **unnecessary** to remove the bullet. Roosevelt recovered **completely,** but for the last seven years of his life the bullet remained a **permanent** part of his body.

Put an X in the box next to the correct answer. After you have completed the exercise, check your answers.

Pick the Main Idea

1. This selection is mainly about
   - ☐ a. a speech that President Theodore Roosevelt made.
   - ☐ b. the result of an assassination attempt on President Theodore Roosevelt.
   - ☐ c. President Theodore Roosevelt's strength and determination.

Observe Supporting Details

2. Theodore Roosevelt was shot
   - ☐ a. before making a speech in Milwaukee.
   - ☐ b. while making a speech in Milwaukee.
   - ☐ c. after making a speech in Milwaukee.

Watch for New Vocabulary

3. As used in this selection, diverted means
   - ☐ a. amused.
   - ☐ b. turned aside.
   - ☐ c. injured.

Explain Cause and Effect

4. President Roosevelt's life was saved by
   - ☐ a. the quick work of his aides.
   - ☐ b. a team of doctors.
   - ☐ c. an eyeglass case in his pocket.

Read to Draw Inferences

5. We may infer that President Roosevelt
   - ☐ a. eventually died from the bullet wound.
   - ☐ b. placed concern with his responsibilities over concern for his welfare.
   - ☐ c. later granted a pardon to John Schrank.

More Spelling Power to You

Look closely at the ten boldface words in the passage. Write each word in a sentence and underline the spelling word. Study the words (see page 103). Then complete the spelling check on the next page. It contains some words from the last lesson and most of the words from this lesson. Therefore, you must review all of the words you have learned before you complete the exercise. Concentrate on words that you previously misspelled.

Check Your Spelling Power

In each group of words, one word is misspelled. On the line, write the letter of the misspelled word.

	a.	b.	c.
1. ________	a. soldier	b. cheif	c. ordinary
2. ________	a. speek	b. speech	c cafeteria
3. ________	a. allways	b. attempt	c. approach
4. ________	a. hankerchief	b. prefer	c. guessed
5. ________	a. buried	b. permitted	c. unecessary
6. ________	a. disagreeable	b. permenent	c. importance
7. ________	a. procede	b. conquer	c. although
8. ________	a. schedule	b. fourty	c. flies
9. ________	a. fortunatly	b. continually	c. valuable
10. ________	a. salary	b. Indian	c. completly

Check your answers in the answer key on page 98. In your notebook, keep a list of the words you misspelled. Study those words until you master them.

Words Often Confused and Misused

Carefully study the meanings of the words and the sample sentences. Complete the exercise below by writing *knew* and *new* in the proper blanks.

knew — The word *knew* is the past tense of the verb *know*.

new — Something that is *new* is very recent or has never existed before.

Although he whistled cheerfully, Aziz **knew,** deep in his heart, that he was frightened.
According to an old saying, a **new** broom sweeps clean.
Every dawn a **new** day begins, Grace **knew.**

1. Nick ________ that after he moved to a ________ neighborhood he would have to make ________ friends.
2. The ________ teacher said that she already ________ the name of every student in class.
3. When the football team failed to score in the first half, the coach ________ that it was time to try some ________ plays.

Now review the Words Often Confused and Misused from previous lessons. They will be included in the Cumulative Review following lesson 16.

Check Your Reading POWER

Some historians **argue** that David Rice Atchinson was the **twelfth** president of the United States—for a day. Here is how they account for that unusual, if somewhat **humorous, occurrence.**

James K. Polk, the **eleventh** president, served his last day in office on Saturday, March 3, 1849. The new president, Zachary Taylor, **preferred** to begin work on Monday, March 5. It therefore appears that for one **calendar** day—Sunday, March 4—the office of the president was **vacant.**

The law expressly stated that when there was **neither** a president nor a vice president in office, the president *pro tempore* of the Senate automatically became president. David Rice Atchinson was president *pro tempore* of the Senate on March 4. Therefore, some historians **consider** him the president for that day.

Put an X in the box next to the correct answer. After you have completed the exercise, check your answers.

Pick the Main Idea

1. This selection is mainly about
   - ☐ a. how Zachary Taylor became president.
   - ☐ b. why some people think David Rice Atchinson was president for a day.
   - ☐ c. the president *pro tempore* of the Senate.

Observe Supporting Details

2. President James K. Polk's last day in office was
   - ☐ a. March 3, 1849.
   - ☐ b. March 4, 1849.
   - ☐ c. March 5, 1849.

Watch for New Vocabulary

3. In the passage, what is the meaning of the word expressly?
   - ☐ a. plainly or clearly
   - ☐ b. quickly or swiftly
   - ☐ c. quietly or softly

Explain Cause and Effect

4. By law, the president *pro tempore* of the Senate became president
   - ☐ a. at the request of the president.
   - ☐ b. when neither a president nor a vice president was in office.
   - ☐ c. as a result of a special election.

Read to Draw Inferences

5. We may infer that
   - ☐ a. most people think of Atchinson as the twelfth president.
   - ☐ b. Atchinson signed several bills into law on the day he was president.
   - ☐ c. Atchinson is not generally considered the twelfth president.

More Spelling Power to You

Look closely at the ten boldface words in the passage. Write each word in a sentence and underline the spelling word. Study the words (see page 103). Then complete the spelling check on the next page. It contains some words from the last lesson and most of the words from this lesson. Therefore, you must review all of the words you have learned before you complete the exercise. Concentrate on words that you previously misspelled.

Check Your Spelling Power

Circle the misspelled word in each of the following pairs of words. Then write the word correctly on the line provided.

________________ 1. favorite vacent

________________ 2. twelvth busy

________________ 3. argue greatful

________________ 4. temperature concider

________________ 5. prefered accompany

________________ 6. neither surprize

________________ 7. occurrance attendance

________________ 8. calender occur

________________ 9. eleventh genuin

________________ 10. humerous balloon

Check your answers in the answer key on page 98. In your notebook, keep a list of the words you misspelled. Study those words until you master them.

Words Often Confused and Misused

Carefully study the meanings of the words and the sample sentences. Complete the exercise below by writing *stationary* and *stationery* in the proper blanks.

stationary The word *stationary* means "not moving" or "not movable."

stationery The word *stationery* means "writing paper" or "writing supplies."

In some rooms in our school, the chairs are **stationary.**
Olga ordered two boxes of white **stationery.**
If the bus remains **stationary** in this traffic jam, I will get to town too late to buy **stationery.**

1. On top of the heavy, ________________ safe in the corner were several sheets of business ________________.
2. Eduardo found a letter written on purple ________________ under the ________________ bleachers in the gym.
3. Because the table was not ________________, when it was bumped the milk spilled over onto the ________________.

Now review the Words Often Confused and Misused from previous lessons. They will be included in the Cumulative Review following lesson 16.

Check Your Reading POWER

During his term in office, President Ulysses S. Grant was once arrested—for speeding.

The incident **occurred** when a police officer observed Grant racing along a Washington, D.C., street in his horse and buggy. After a long chase, the officer managed to **seize** the horse's bridle and bring the animal to a halt.

The discovery that the wrongdoer was the president served to **embarrass** the officer. He started to **apologize** and was reluctant to arrest the dignitary. Grant, however, acted in a completely **honorable** manner. He did not use the presidency as a **defense,** nor did he **hesitate** to assume **responsibility**. He insisted that the officer **pursue** the arrest. Because he did **exceed** the speed limit, Grant was later fined twenty dollars for the offense.

Put an X in the box next to the correct answer. After you have completed the exercise, check your answers.

Pick the Main Idea

1. This selection is mainly about
   - ☐ a. how a police officer became embarrassed.
   - ☐ b. how President Grant was once arrested for speeding.
   - ☐ c. the fine that President Grant received for speeding.

Observe Supporting Details

2. After the officer spoke to Grant, the president
   - ☐ a. used the presidency as a defense.
   - ☐ b. refused to accept responsibility.
   - ☐ c. insisted that the officer make the arrest.

Watch for New Vocabulary

3. What is the meaning of the word dignitary?
   - ☐ a. person of high position
   - ☐ b. someone who is not well-known
   - ☐ c. gentle or kind

Explain Cause and Effect

4. The officer was able to stop the horse and buggy by
   - ☐ a. blowing a whistle.
   - ☐ b. chasing the animal until it grew tired.
   - ☐ c. grabbing the horse's bridle.

Read to Draw Inferences

5. We may infer that at the time Grant was president
   - ☐ a. police officers were more thoughtful than they are today.
   - ☐ b. presidents traveled with less protection than they do today.
   - ☐ c. there were many automobiles on the road.

More Spelling Power to You

Look closely at the ten boldface words in the passage. Write each word in a sentence and underline the spelling word. Study the words (see page 103). Then complete the spelling check on the next page. It contains some words from the last lesson and most of the words from this lesson. Therefore, you must review all of the words you have learned before you complete the exercise. Concentrate on words that you previously misspelled.

Check Your Spelling Power

Circle the misspelled word in each of the following groups of words. Then write the word correctly on the line provided.

____________	1.	hezitate	million	often	across
____________	2.	weigh	sieze	probably	around
____________	3.	anxious	apologize	prefer	argu
____________	4.	appreciate	exhibit	honerable	occasion
____________	5.	persue	extremely	banquet	restaurant
____________	6.	embarass	having	library	all right
____________	7.	speech	responsability	courageous	forward
____________	8.	generally	until	twelfth	defence
____________	9.	written	fortunately	occured	therefore
____________	10.	excede	unnecessary	handkerchief	business

Check your answers in the answer key on page 98. In your notebook, keep a list of the words you misspelled. Study those words until you master them.

Words Often Confused and Misused

Carefully study the meanings of the words and the sample sentences. Complete the exercise below by writing *all together* and *altogether* in the proper blanks.

all together The words *all together* mean "everybody or everything together in the same place."

altogether The word *altogether* means "entirely."

As soon as the group was **all together,** Chung snapped the picture.
His idea of how it should be done is **altogether** different from my own.
If we work **all together,** it's **altogether** possible that we'll finish on time.

1. I think Thanksgiving is ____________ delightful, because that's the time when my family is ____________.
2. The conductor called us ____________ to say that the music was ____________ too difficult to learn by next week.
3. Although the farm was ____________ destroyed by the fire, the farmer got his horses ____________ and rushed them to safety.

Now review the Words Often Confused and Misused from previous lessons. They will be included in the Cumulative Review following lesson 16.

Lesson 16

Check Your Reading POWER

Here is another interesting story about President Theodore (Teddy) Roosevelt. In 1902 Roosevelt went on a bear-hunting trip. On the **fourth** day, a bear cub made its **appearance.** It was not very tall and was also small in girth. The president's friends chased the bear for **approximately** a mile. Then they tied it to a tree and asked the president to shoot it. "I cannot kill this helpless animal," Roosevelt **answered.**

A storekeeper in Brooklyn saw a cartoon that described the incident. He started to make toy bears. It was his **opinion** that sales would be **excellent.** He wrote to President Teddy Roosevelt and asked for permission to call the toys "Teddy's Bears." Roosevelt was glad to **accommodate.**

There is no **doubt** that the shopkeeper's **judgment** was **certainly** right. Millions of "teddy bears" have been sold over the years.

Put an X in the box next to the correct answer. After you have completed the exercise, check your answers.

Pick the Main Idea

1. This selection is mainly about
   - ☐ a. why it is cruel to kill animals.
   - ☐ b. how the teddy bear got its name.
   - ☐ c. the life of Theodore Roosevelt.

Observe Supporting Details

2. How did the storekeeper learn about the bear-hunting incident?
   - ☐ a. from a cartoon
   - ☐ b. from a magazine story
   - ☐ c. by hearing about it on the radio

Watch for New Vocabulary

3. What is the meaning of the word girth?
   - ☐ a. height
   - ☐ b. age
   - ☐ c. measurement around a body

Explain Cause and Effect

4. Roosevelt refused to kill the bear because
   - ☐ a. it was completely helpless.
   - ☐ b. he was afraid of the animal.
   - ☐ c. he decided to give it to a zoo.

Read to Draw Inferences

5. This passage suggests that
   - ☐ a. the president seldom listened to his friends.
   - ☐ b. Roosevelt never went hunting again.
   - ☐ c. teddy bears are extremely popular toys.

More Spelling Power to You

Look closely at the ten boldface words in the passage. Write each word in a sentence and underline the spelling word. Study the words (see page 103). Then complete the spelling check on the next page. It contains some words from the last lesson and most of the words from this lesson. Therefore, you must review all of the words you have learned before you complete the exercise. Concentrate on words that you previously misspelled.

Check Your Spelling Power

Underline the misspelled word in each sentence. Then write the word correctly on the line provided.

_______________ 1. Babe Ruth finished an absolutely glorious career by hitting a home run in his last appearence at bat.

_______________ 2. Consuelo ansered the questions by using the books she found in the library.

_______________ 3. I have a different opinion about how the terrible accident ocurred.

_______________ 4. *The Red Badge of Courage,* written in 1895, certanly offers a brilliant description of a person's feelings during a war.

_______________ 5. There is no dout that Kim's explanation makes sense.

_______________ 6. John James Audubon, an excellent artist, usally preferred to draw pictures of the birds he'd been studying.

_______________ 7. I must apolagize for making an error in judgment.

_______________ 8. The clerk said, "I believe we will be able to acommodate you if we receive your request this week."

_______________ 9. If people keep coming to our games, attendance should far exceed that of last season and reach approximitely two thousand.

_______________ 10. Her fourth attempt was a bit awkward; therefor Ann did not get a perfect score in diving.

Check your answers in the answer key on page 98. In your notebook, keep a list of the words you misspelled. Study those words until you master them.

Words Often Confused and Misused

Carefully study the meanings of the words and the sample sentences. Complete the exercise below by writing *brake* and *break* in the proper blanks.

brake The word *brake* refers to "anything that slows or stops a moving vehicle."

break The word *break* means "to shatter or smash."

Every car needs a good emergency **brake.**
A bull in a china shop is bound to **break** something.
If you ride a bicycle without a **brake,** you might **break** some bones.

1. The __________ on my scooter happened to __________.

2. Don't __________ the law; be sure that the __________ on your car is working.

3. When the __________ on her bicycle failed to operate, Rita was lucky she didn't __________ her arm.

Now review the Words Often Confused and Misused from lessons 1–16. They will be included in the Cumulative Review that begins on the next page.

Cumulative Review of Units 1–4

A. In each of the following groups of words, one word is misspelled. Circle the misspelled word. Then write the word correctly on the line to the left.

______ 1. completely
exceede
hesitate

______ 2. embarras
surprise
sense

______ 3. suppose
beginning
quantaty

______ 4. importance
praferred
forty

______ 5. occurrence
balloon
humerous

______ 6. Indian
critacism
recognize

______ 7. relief
opinon
terrible

______ 8. across
dapendent
interrupt

______ 9. judgement
library
toward

______ 10. occasion
biggest
accomodate

B. Fill in the blanks in the words to create words that are spelled correctly. Then write the words on the lines to the left.

______ 11. d __ scribe

______ 12. con __ ider

______ 13. appear __ nce

______ 14. exist __ nce

______ 15. exc __ ll __nt

______ 16. ap __ l __ gize

______ 17. caf __ t __ ria

______ 18. approx __ m __ tely

______ 19. perm __ n __ n t

______ 20. r __ spons __ b __ l __ ty

C. The letters *ie* or *ei* are missing from each of the words below. Fill in the blanks in each word to spell the word correctly. Then write the word on the line to the left.

______ 21. ch __ __ f

______ 22. n __ __ ther

______ 23. s __ __ ze

______ 24. bel __ __ ve

______ 25. w __ __ gh

D. In each of the following sentences, one of the four underlined words is misspelled. Circle the misspelled word. Then write the word correctly on the line before the sentence.

______ 26. In an <u>absolutely</u> <u>brilliant</u> <u>speech</u>, Mark Antony said that Caesar's murderers were all <u>honerable</u> men.

______ 27. Please check your <u>skedule</u> to see if you can meet me on the <u>fourth</u>, the <u>eleventh</u>, or the <u>twelfth</u>.

_______________ 28. Myrna eventually was able to conquer her fear of high places; now she often flys without concern.

_______________ 29. Almost nothing is impossible if you continually try untill you succeed.

_______________ 30. Without doubt, Darren's attendance is truely extraordinary.

_______________ 31. When the temprature is extremely high, people always ask, "Is it hot enough for you?"

_______________ 32. You will discover that it is certainly better to give than to recieve—especially if you are having a fight.

_______________ 33. The office is usually busy, but if you arrive early you will probably be able to speek to Mr. James.

_______________ 34. When the tightrope walker accidentally slipped, there was great excitement; fortunately, she was alright.

_______________ 35. The novel is still interesting and fascinating, althogh it was written many years ago.

E. Each of the following sentences contains two words in parentheses. Underline the one that makes the sentence correct. Then write the word on the line to the left.

_______________ 36. Once, many years ago, our old car was (knew, new).

_______________ 37. A sign in large letters said, "Watch (your, you're) hat and coat."

_______________ 38. When we went on vacation, it rained all (weak, week).

_______________ 39. The Pacific Ocean is larger (than, then) the Atlantic Ocean.

_______________ 40. What time is it in Paris when (its, it's) ten o'clock in New York?

_______________ 41. The waiter said, "Don't mention that there's a fly in your soup or everyone else will want one (to, too, two)."

_______________ 42. In the morning, I can't decide (weather, whether) to get out of bed on the left side or the right side.

_______________ 43. The conductor asked the orchestra, "Are you (all ready, already) to play?"

_______________ 44. I want to write a letter on your fancy (stationary, stationery).

_______________ 45. On stage Joel is showy and loud; offstage he is (quiet, quite).

_______________ 46. Please (accept, except) our thanks for a job well done.

_______________ 47. It is likely that their concert will (brake, break) all records.

_______________ 48. Are you the girl (whose, who's) dog ate my book?

_______________ 49. I thought I might (loose, lose) the race when I saw that I was last.

_______________ 50. The Mississippi River flows (threw, through) ten states.

Unit 5

Literary Favorites

When you have completed this unit, you will have mastered 200 of the words that are most frequently misspelled and 41 words that are commonly confused and misused.

Check Your Reading POWER

You **remember** Alice, of course. She is the girl who **dropped** into a hole while **running** after a white rabbit that was **hurrying** along. What followed were the adventures of Alice in Wonderland.

Before Alice returned home from Wonderland, she made the **acquaintance** of many **weird** and wonderful creatures. Among them were the Mad Hatter, the Mock Turtle, and the Queen of Hearts.

Alice's creator, Lewis Carroll, was a **professor** of mathematics at a **college** in England. Carroll wrote *Alice in Wonderland* **especially** for a little girl named Alice Liddell, the daughter of a friend. He made up the story of Alice one day in 1862, while they were **picnicking.** Over time he began to embellish, or add details to, the story. Three years later, *Alice's Adventures in Wonderland* was published. It has long been a favorite children's book.

Put an X in the box next to the correct answer. After you have completed the exercise, check your answers.

Pick the Main Idea

1. This selection is mainly about
   - ☐ a. Alice Liddell.
   - ☐ b. the Mad Hatter.
   - ☐ c. *Alice in Wonderland* and its author.

Observe Supporting Details

2. Lewis Carroll wrote *Alice in Wonderland*
   - ☐ a. for some students at a college.
   - ☐ b. for the daughter of a friend.
   - ☐ c. because he needed money.

Watch for New Vocabulary

3. As used in this selection, what does the word embellish mean?
   - ☐ a. to go on a picnic
   - ☐ b. to go to a strange land
   - ☐ c. to add details to a story

Explain Cause and Effect

4. Alice's adventures in Wonderland began when she
   - ☐ a. dropped into a hole while chasing a rabbit.
   - ☐ b. met the Queen of Hearts.
   - ☐ c. went to a college in England.

Read to Draw Inferences

5. We may infer that *Alice in Wonderland* was first published in
   - ☐ a. 1862.
   - ☐ b. 1865.
   - ☐ c. 1859.

More Spelling Power to You

Look closely at the ten boldface words in the passage. Write each word in a sentence and underline the spelling word. Study the words (see page 103). Then complete the spelling check on the next page. It contains some words from the last lesson and most of the words from this lesson. Therefore, you must review all of the words you have learned before you complete the exercise. Concentrate on words that you previously misspelled.

Check Your Spelling Power

In each group of words, one word is misspelled. On the line, write the letter of the misspelled word.

	a.	b.	c.
1. ________	a. occur	b. proffessor	c. across
2. ________	a. dropped	b. permited	c. genuine
3. ________	a. appreciate	b. happened	c. colledge
4. ________	a. wierd	b. soldier	c. before
5. ________	a. especialy	b. buried	c. prefer
6. ________	a. akwaintance	b. ordinary	c. defense
7. ________	a. embarrass	b. consider	c. picknicking
8. ________	a. remember	b. favrite	c. conquer
9. ________	a. around	b. runing	c. written
10. ________	a. hurryng	b. valuable	c. similar

Check your answers in the answer key on page 99. In your notebook, keep a list of the words you misspelled. Study those words until you master them.

Words Often Confused and Misused

Carefully study the meanings of the words and the sample sentences. Complete the exercise below by writing *hear* and *here* in the proper blanks.

hear The word *hear* means "to take in sounds through the ear."

here The word *here* means "in this place."

When did you **hear** the good news?
Let's all meet **here** on Thursday.
Speak into the microphone so that everyone **here** will be able to **hear** you.

1. As soon as you ________ the starter's gun, race from ________ to the finish line.
2. Perhaps we should camp ________, for I ________ that rain is on the way.
3. I was sorry to ________ of his illness, but I realized that something was the matter when I did not see him ________.

Now review the Words Often Confused and Misused from previous lessons. They will be included in the Cumulative Review that follows lesson 24.

Check Your Reading POWER

Washington Irving was the first American **author** to earn a living by **writing.** Famous in his day, today Irving is probably best known as the creator of the fictional character Rip Van Winkle.

Rip is one of Irving's most popular **heroes.** In the story entitled "Rip Van Winkle," Rip takes a nap that lasts for twenty years. When he falls asleep in 1756, the thirteen American colonies are under the domination of King George of England. When he awakes two decades later, the colonies have become a **democracy, independent** of England.

Rip, of course, was in a **vacuum** while that great change was taking place, and he awakes **ignorant** of what happened during his **absence.** He doesn't **realize** that while he was sleeping he became a citizen of the new United States of America. He is so confused by the changes he finds around him that he feels like a visitor in a **foreign** land.

Put an X in the box next to the correct answer. After you have completed the exercise, check your answers.

Pick the Main Idea

1. This selection is mainly about
   - ☐ a. England's colonization of North America.
   - ☐ b. Rip Van Winkle.
   - ☐ c. how the colonies became independent of England.

Observe Supporting Details

2. Washington Irving was the first American author to
   - ☐ a. earn a living by writing.
   - ☐ b. become a citizen of the United States.
   - ☐ c. fight for the colonies.

Watch for New Vocabulary

3. What is the meaning of the word domination?
   - ☐ a. cruelty
   - ☐ b. flag
   - ☐ c. rule

Explain Cause and Effect

4. Today, Irving's reputation is based mainly on
   - ☐ a. one story he wrote.
   - ☐ b. his novels of adventure.
   - ☐ c. his support of democracy.

Read to Draw Inferences

5. If someone calls you a Rip Van Winkle, that person is probably suggesting that you
   - ☐ a. enjoy working very hard.
   - ☐ b. are very bright.
   - ☐ c. are out of touch with what's happening around you.

More Spelling Power to You

Look closely at the ten boldface words in the passage. Write each word in a sentence and underline the spelling word. Study the words (see page 103). Then complete the spelling check on the next page. It contains some words from the last lesson and most of the words from this lesson. Therefore, you must review all of the words you have learned before you complete the exercise. Concentrate on words that you previously misspelled.

Check Your Spelling Power

Circle the misspelled word in each of the following pairs of words. Then write the word correctly on the line provided.

____________	1. writting professor	____________	6. suppose democrasy
____________	2. salary independant	____________	7. vacum straight
____________	3. payed realize	____________	8. ignorant especialy
____________	4. author remembar	____________	9. existance foreign
____________	5. heros library	____________	10. absense impossible

Check your answers in the answer key on page 99. In your notebook, keep a list of the words you misspelled. Study those words until you master them.

Words Often Confused and Misused

Carefully study the meanings of the words and the sample sentences. Complete the exercise below by writing *shone* and *shown* in the proper blanks.

shone — The word *shone* is the past tense of *shine.*

shown — The word *shown* is the past participle of *show,* meaning "to reveal or make known."

From the first day of our vacation, the sun has not shone.
How many times has he shown you his stamp collection?
When she had shown us how the trick was done, the magician's eyes shone with delight.

1. The moon __________ down on the pyramids that our guide had just __________ us.

2. When her project was __________ to the class, Tanya's eyes __________ with delight.

3. Because the light __________ into the room, the movie was not __________.

Now review the Words Often Confused and Misused from previous lessons. They will be included in the Cumulative Review following lesson 24.

Lesson 19

Check Your Reading POWER

The novel *Don Quixote* is one of the masterpieces of world **literature.** Written by Miguel de Cervantes, its main **character** is the wonderful Don Quixote.

Cervantes' story recounts the tale of a middle-aged landowner who sees himself as a knight of old. It tells how he dresses in armor and **announces** that he is Don Quixote of La Mancha. He sets out, **committed** to battle for justice, with his faithful companion, Sancho Panza.

A man of great **conscience,** Don Quixote attempts to **achieve** victory over evil. He is fearless, **stubborn,** courageous, and proud. Sometimes he is also silly. Sancho Panza, on the other hand, is always **sensible** and cautious. The two have many **amusing** adventures **together.** In one famous episode, Don Quixote attacks a group of windmills, which he thinks are giants.

Put an X in the box next to the correct answer. After you have completed the exercise, check your answers.

Pick the Main Idea

1. This selection is mainly about
   - ☐ a. Sancho Panza.
   - ☐ b. Don Quixote.
   - ☐ c. Miguel de Cervantes.

Observe Supporting Details

2. Don Quixote was a
   - ☐ a. knight of old.
   - ☐ b. Spanish landowner.
   - ☐ c. famous writer.

Watch for New Vocabulary

3. What is the meaning of the word recounts?
   - ☐ a. counts again
   - ☐ b. hears
   - ☐ c. tells

Explain Cause and Effect

4. Don Quixote attacked some windmills because he
   - ☐ a. thought they were giants.
   - ☐ b. thought his enemies were hiding inside them.
   - ☐ c. hated windmills.

Read to Draw Inferences

5. We may infer that Don Quixote
   - ☐ a. was a coward.
   - ☐ b. had a lively imagination.
   - ☐ c. always listened to Sancho Panza.

More Spelling Power to You

Look closely at the ten boldface words in the passage. Write each word in a sentence and underline the spelling word. Study the words (see page 103). Then complete the spelling check on the next page. It contains some words from the last lesson and most of the words from this lesson. Therefore, you must review all of the words you have learned before you complete the exercise. Concentrate on words that you previously misspelled.

Check Your Spelling Power

Circle the misspelled word in each of the following groups of words. Then write the word correctly on the line provided.

______ 1. amuseing
writing
losing
making

______ 2. acquaintance
twelfth
until
litrature

______ 3. stubborn
auther
usually
forty

______ 4. college
source
anounces
familiar

______ 5. concience
picnicking
vacuum
honorable

______ 6. height
achieve
sandwich
facinating

______ 7. heroes
ignorent
weird
together

______ 8. sensable
independent
pursue
running

______ 9. hurrying
democracy
commited
equipped

______ 10. calendar
charactor
absence
necessary

Check your answers in the answer key on page 99. In your notebook, keep a list of the words you misspelled. Study those words until you master them.

Words Often Confused and Misused

Carefully study the meanings of the words and the sample sentences. Complete the exercise below by writing *peace* and *piece* in the proper blanks.

peace The word *peace* means "calmness and stillness" or "absence of war."

piece The word *piece* means "a part of something."

The two countries had always lived together in **peace.**
May I have a very small **piece** of cake?
Since he received that **piece** of bad news, he has known no **peace.**

1. The ______ treaty was written on a ______ of white paper.
2. Audrey munched on a ______ of apple and happily enjoyed the ______ and quiet of the country.
3. A dispute over a tiny ______ of land suddenly broke the ______.

Now review the Words Often Confused and Misused from previous lessons. They will be included in the Cumulative Review following lesson 24.

Lesson 20

Check Your Reading POWER

An **ancient** Greek myth tells the sad story of Orpheus and Eurydice. Orpheus was a poet and musician who fell in love with the beautiful Eurydice and married her.

Soon after the **marriage,** death came like a **thief** and took Eurydice. How Orpheus did **grieve!** Filled with **despair,** he decided to **descend** to the land of the dead to try to get her back. There he met Pluto, who ruled that dark domain.

Orpheus begged for Eurydice's return. He played his lyre for Pluto. So **beautiful** was his song and so **sincerely** did he plead that he was able to **persuade** Pluto to make a bargain. "Eurydice may follow behind you to the land of the living," said Pluto. "But if you look back at her before you arrive, she will **disappear.**"

Joyfully, Orpheus led Eurydice to the land of the living. As he stepped into the sunlight, he turned to welcome her. But Eurydice was still in the gloom. As soon as Orpheus glimpsed her shadowy form, she disappeared, uttering only a faint "Farewell."

Put an X in the box next to the correct answer. After you have completed the exercise, check your answers.

Pick the Main Idea

1. This selection is mainly about
   - ☐ a. the story of Orpheus and Eurydice.
   - ☐ b. the ancient Greeks.
   - ☐ c. ancient Greek myths.

Observe Supporting Details

2. Orpheus was a wonderful
   - ☐ a. writer.
   - ☐ b. magician.
   - ☐ c. musician.

Watch for New Vocabulary

3. What is the meaning of the word domain?
   - ☐ a. kingdom
   - ☐ b. sleep
   - ☐ c. rock

Explain Cause and Effect

4. Orpheus lost Eurydice forever because
   - ☐ a. she no longer loved him.
   - ☐ b. Pluto refused to let her return to the land of the living.
   - ☐ c. he looked back at her.

Read to Draw Inferences

5. After Eurydice disappeared, Orpheus probably
   - ☐ a. went back to talk to Pluto again.
   - ☐ b. was overcome with sorrow.
   - ☐ c. believed that Eurydice would return one day.

More Spelling Power to You

Look closely at the ten boldface words in the passage. Write each word in a sentence and underline the spelling word. Study the words (see page 103). Then complete the spelling check on the next page. It contains some words from the last lesson and most of the words from this lesson. Therefore, you must review all of the words you have learned before you complete the exercise. Concentrate on words that you previously misspelled.

Check Your Spelling Power

Underline the misspelled word in each sentence. Then write the word correctly on the line provided.

________________ 1. The victim of the crime was able to recognize the theif at once.

________________ 2. On Sunday, they will celebrate the fourth anniversary of their marrage.

________________ 3. After his team committed its sixth error, the coach was filled with a sense of dispair.

________________ 4. On the walls of the cave you will discover ancient paintings that are very intresting.

________________ 5. Please accept my apology; I am sincerly sorry for the confusion that occurred.

________________ 6. Moments after the banquet ended, the guests headed toward the exit and began to disapear.

________________ 7. This is the most beautyful work of literature I have ever read.

________________ 8. In case of fire, remember to decend the stairs and proceed directly to the street.

________________ 9. It is certainly not unusual to greive over the loss of a pet.

________________ 10. As a leader, she was known for excellent judgement and for the ability to persuade her followers.

Check your answers in the answer key on page 99. In your notebook, keep a list of the words you misspelled. Study those words until you master them.

Words Often Confused and Misused

Carefully study the meanings of the words and the sample sentences. Complete the exercise below by writing *advice* and *advise* in the proper blanks.

advice — The noun *advice* (ad-VICE) means "an opinion or suggestion about what should be done."

advise — The verb *advise* (ad-VIZE) means "to give an opinion or advice."

Thank you for your excellent advice.
If you wish to be a better tennis player, I advise you to practice more.
The judge said, "I advise you to follow my advice."

1. I'd ________________ you to speak to a lawyer for ________________.

2. "We can ________________ you," said the coach, "but you must decide whether or not to follow our ________________."

3. Few things are as valuable and inexpensive as good ________________; I ________________ you to remember that.

Now review the Words Often Confused and Misused from previous lessons. They will be included in the Cumulative Review that follows lesson 24.

Unit 6

When you have completed this unit, you will have mastered 240 of the words that are most frequently misspelled and 49 words that are commonly confused and misused.

Check Your Reading POWER

Draw an **imaginary** line from Florida to Puerto Rico to Bermuda and back to Florida. That area of the Atlantic is known as the Bermuda Triangle. For more than a hundred years, ships and planes have seemingly vanished within that **boundary.**

On December 5, 1945, for example, five U.S. Navy planes left Florida on a training mission. An hour later, all the planes began to **experience** problems. Their compasses were <u>incapable</u> of giving an **accurate** reading. The **lieutenant** in charge of the mission radioed the control tower that they were lost.

A rescue plane **carrying** emergency **equipment** was dispatched at once. Neither it nor the other five planes were seen or heard from **again.**

There is no completely **satisfactory** explanation for the **tragedy.** But this much can be said: all the planes were lost in the Bermuda Triangle.

Put an X in the box next to the correct answer. After you have completed the exercise, check your answers.

Pick the Main Idea

1. This selection is mainly about
   - ☐ a. why ships and planes have been lost near Bermuda.
   - ☐ b. a famous air rescue.
   - ☐ c. an event that took place in the Bermuda Triangle.

Observe Supporting Details

2. The Bermuda Triangle is
   - ☐ a. an imaginary line over Florida.
   - ☐ b. an area in the Atlantic Ocean.
   - ☐ c. the area between Puerto Rico and Bermuda.

Watch for New Vocabulary

3. What is the meaning of the word <u>incapable</u>?
   - ☐ a. able
   - ☐ b. unable
   - ☐ c. false

Explain Cause and Effect

4. What caused the tragedy in the Bermuda Triangle?
   - ☐ a. A sudden storm arose.
   - ☐ b. The planes ran out of gas.
   - ☐ c. There is no completely satisfactory explanation.

Read to Draw Inferences

5. This selection suggests that
   - ☐ a. strange forces may be at work in the Bermuda Triangle.
   - ☐ b. compasses often give readings that are not accurate.
   - ☐ c. the Navy pilots were not following orders.

More Spelling Power to You

Look closely at the ten boldface words in the passage. Write each word in a sentence and underline the spelling word. Study the words (see page 103). Then complete the spelling check on the next page. It contains some words from the last lesson and most of the words from this lesson. Therefore, you must review all of the words you have learned before you complete the exercise. Concentrate on words that you previously misspelled.

Check Your Spelling Power

In each group of words, one word is misspelled. On the line, write the letter of the misspelled word.

	a.	b.	c.
1. ________	a. again	b. ammong	c. amusing
2. ________	a. boundry	b. career	c. disappear
3. ________	a. ache	b. sincerely	c. experiance
4. ________	a. leutenant	b. foreign	c. descend
5. ________	a. announce	b. satisfactary	c. exhibit
6. ________	a. beautiful	b. acurate	c. conscience
7. ________	a. character	b. imaginery	c. nonsense
8. ________	a. realise	b. heroes	c. tragedy
9. ________	a. guessed	b. marriage	c. equiptment
10. ________	a. carrying	b. stuborn	c. despair

Check your answers in the answer key on page 99. In your notebook, keep a list of the words you misspelled. Study those words until you master them.

Words Often Confused and Misused

Carefully study the meanings of the words and the sample sentences. Complete the exercise below by writing *principal* and *principle* in the proper blanks.

principal The word *principal* means "most important or main." It may also mean "the leader or head of a school."

principle The word *principle* means "a basic rule, truth, or law."

Our **principal** was the **principal** speaker.
She believes in the **principle** that honesty is the best policy.
The **principal** parts of the verb were listed in the chapter on the **principles** of grammar.

1. Mr. Hernandez, the ____________________, showed the new students the ____________________ parts of the school.
2. The ____________________ of free speech was the ____________________ subject of the talk.
3. The ____________________ asked us to state one ____________________ that we believe in.

Now review the Words Often Confused and Misused from previous lessons. They will be included in the Cumulative Review that follows lesson 24.

Lesson 22

Check Your Reading POWER

The "**eighth** wonder of the world" was discovered in 1869 on a farm in Cardiff, New York. Workers digging a well there uncovered a large stone figure buried in the ground. It was ten feet long and weighed three thousand pounds. While opinion about the find was **divided,** some "scientists" said that it was the petrified remains of an ancient giant man.

When people **heard** the news, they **immediately** rushed to the **scene.** They paid fifty cents each for the **privilege** of seeing the giant.

Two months later, some facts about the Cardiff Giant came to light. The figure had been carved from stone by stonecutters in Chicago. The huge statue had then been **transferred** to the farm, where it was buried in the earth. It was all part of a get-rich-quick **scheme planned** by an **individual** named George Hull. The "eighth wonder of the world" had been a giant <u>hoax</u>.

Put an X in the box next to the correct answer. After you have completed the exercise, check your answers.

Pick the Main Idea

1. This selection is mainly about
   - ☐ a. the Cardiff Giant.
   - ☐ b. George Hull.
   - ☐ c. the greatest hoaxes of all time.

Observe Supporting Details

2. The Cardiff Giant was
   - ☐ a. the remains of an early giant man.
   - ☐ b. ten feet long.
   - ☐ c. carved from stone in New York.

Watch for New Vocabulary

3. What is the meaning of the word <u>hoax</u>?
   - ☐ a. trick
   - ☐ b. carver
   - ☐ c. robbery

Explain Cause and Effect

4. People rushed to Cardiff, New York, to
   - ☐ a. look for other stone giants.
   - ☐ b. meet with some scientists.
   - ☐ c. see a stone giant.

Read to Draw Inferences

5. The quotation marks around the word *scientists* suggest that
   - ☐ a. the people weren't really scientists.
   - ☐ b. the scientists were very well known.
   - ☐ c. scientists are never wrong.

More Spelling Power to You

Look closely at the ten boldface words in the passage. Write each word in a sentence and underline the spelling word. Study the words (see page 103). Then complete the spelling check on the next page. It contains some words from the last lesson and most of the words from this lesson. Therefore, you must review all of the words you have learned before you complete the exercise. Concentrate on words that you previously misspelled.

Check Your Spelling Power

Circle the misspelled word in each of the following pairs of words. Then write the word correctly on the line provided.

_______________ 1. heard
anceint

_______________ 2. devided
imaginary

_______________ 3. imediately
experience

_______________ 4. trully
planned

_______________ 5. skeme
lieutenant

_______________ 6. boundary
priviledge

_______________ 7. eigth
attendance

_______________ 8. scene
tradgedy

_______________ 9. transfered
equipment

_______________ 10. grievous
individuel

Check your answers in the answer key on page 99. In your notebook, keep a list of the words you misspelled. Study those words until you master them.

Words Often Confused and Misused

Carefully study the meanings of the words and the sample sentences. Complete the exercise below by writing *past* and *passed* in the proper blanks.

past The word *past* means "just finished or ended." It sometimes refers to "a time gone by."

passed The word *passed* is the past tense of the verb "to pass," which means "to go by," "to use," or "to be successful on a test or in a class."

For the **past** month, the weather has been beautiful.
Putting on a burst of speed, Sue **passed** the other runners.
Adele **passed** all the subjects she took this **past** year.

1. Jason _______________ the hours reading about great scientists of the _______________.

2. In a _______________ race, Raul _______________ all the other runners.

3. Now that the final exam was _______________, Gloria was anxious to know if she had _______________ chemistry.

Now review the Words Often Confused and Misused from previous lessons. They will be included in the Cumulative Review that follows lesson 24.

Lesson 23

Check Your Reading POWER

On a **pleasant** day in 1872, the British ship *Dei Gratia* was on its way to Spain. When the *Dei Gratia* was **almost** six hundred miles off the coast of Gibraltar, the lookout became **conscious** of a ship in the distance. It seemed to be just drifting randomly on the quiet sea.

The *Dei Gratia's* **captain** thought that perhaps the ship needed **assistance.** So he ordered some of his men to board it at once. They discovered that the name of the ship was the *Mary Celeste*. It was **evidently** in excellent condition—clean, dry, and well stocked with food. Its cargo was untouched. There were no **noticeable** signs of struggle or flight. Everything seemed normal—*but there was no one on board!*

The men searched the ship **thoroughly.** They were looking for a clue to what had happened to the crew. But nothing they found would **yield** an answer. To this day, no one **really** knows what happened to the passengers and crew of the *Mary Celeste*.

Put an X in the box next to the correct answer. After you have completed the exercise, check your answers.

Pick the Main Idea

1. This selection is mainly about
   - ☐ a. the mystery of the *Mary Celeste*.
   - ☐ b. the captain of the British ship *Dei Gratia*.
   - ☐ c. the dangers of sailing ships.

Observe Supporting Details

2. Which one of the following was true of the *Mary Celeste*?
   - ☐ a. There were signs of a struggle on the boat.
   - ☐ b. The ship was in poor condition.
   - ☐ c. The boat was well stocked with food.

Watch for New Vocabulary

3. What is the meaning of the word randomly?
   - ☐ a. silently
   - ☐ b. aimlessly
   - ☐ c. quickly

Explain Cause and Effect

4. The captain ordered some men to board the *Mary Celeste* because he
   - ☐ a. knew that there was no one on the ship.
   - ☐ b. thought that the ship needed help.
   - ☐ c. was following orders to search the boat.

Read to Draw Inferences

5. We may infer that the passengers and crew of the *Mary Celeste* had not been lost in a storm, because the
   - ☐ a. boat was found on a pleasant day.
   - ☐ b. ship's cargo was untouched.
   - ☐ c. boat was dry and in good condition.

More Spelling Power to You

Look closely at the ten boldface words in the passage. Write each word in a sentence and underline the spelling word. Study the words (see page 103). Then complete the spelling check on the next page. It contains some words from the last lesson and most of the words from this lesson. Therefore, you must review all of the words you have learned before you complete the exercise. Concentrate on words that you previously misspelled.

Check Your Spelling Power

Circle the misspelled word in each of the following groups of words. Then write the word correctly on the line provided.

_______________ **1.** immediately
realy
transferred
terrible

_______________ **2.** allmost
all right
although
always

_______________ **3.** college
privilege
captin
accurate

_______________ **4.** scene
scheme
concious
absence

_______________ **5.** eighth
throughly
extraordinary
vacuum

_______________ **6.** asistence
especially
stubborn
accompany

_______________ **7.** yield
acheive
busy
divided

_______________ **8.** literature
enough
carryng
evidently

_______________ **9.** pleasent
appearance
individual
doubt

_______________ **10.** using
equipment
noticable
tragedy

Check your answers in the answer key on page 99. In your notebook, keep a list of the words you misspelled. Study those words until you master them.

Words Often Confused and Misused

Carefully study the meanings of the words and the sample sentences. Complete the exercise below by writing *miner* and *minor* in the proper blanks.

miner The word *miner* means "a person who works in a mine."

minor The word *minor* means "less important or smaller." It may also mean "a person who is not yet of legal age."

The work of a **miner** is often very difficult.
The lawyer raised a **minor** objection because the key witness was still a **minor.**
He could not be employed as a **miner** until he was no longer a **minor.**

1. Julio's paper about the life of a coal __________ contained only a few __________ typing errors.
2. Although she was still a __________ and could not yet vote, Leah did not consider voting a __________ responsibility.
3. As a young man, George worked as a __________ in the hills of West Virginia, but years later he gained a bit of fame as a __________ poet.

Now review the Words Often Confused and Misused from previous lessons. They will be included in the Cumulative Review that follows lesson 24.

Lesson 24

Check Your Reading POWER

In remote parts of China, villagers have sometimes told of seeing a hairy, two-legged beast more than seven feet tall. The creature is **referred** to as the wild man, or Ye Ren.

According to reports, Ye Ren walks upright, has thick hair all over its body, and does not **possess** a tail. It is not afraid of fire and has great **physical strength.** Through the years, there have been many **separate** sightings of Ye Ren. However, the fact that it **actually** exists has never **definitely** been proved.

Scientists would like to capture Ye Ren in the flesh—or at least on film. With that intention, they have made several trips to the jungles of China. Those excursions, however, have not **benefited science** much. So far, footprints eighteen inches long are the only signs anyone has found of the **mysterious** Ye Ren.

Put an X in the box next to the correct answer. After you have completed the exercise, check your answers.

Pick the Main Idea

1. This selection is mainly about
   - ☐ a. scientists around the world.
   - ☐ b. villagers in China.
   - ☐ c. Ye Ren.

Observe Supporting Details

2. According to reports, Ye Ren
   - ☐ a. has great strength.
   - ☐ b. has a tail.
   - ☐ c. is afraid of fire.

Watch for New Vocabulary

3. What is the meaning of the word excursions?
   - ☐ a. sightings
   - ☐ b. trips
   - ☐ c. films

Explain Cause and Effect

4. Scientists have traveled to the jungles of China in order to
   - ☐ a. meet with the leaders of the country.
   - ☐ b. take movies of the countryside.
   - ☐ c. look for Ye Ren.

Read to Draw Inferences

5. If there is a Ye Ren, we may infer that it
   - ☐ a. has very small feet.
   - ☐ b. stays hidden most of the time.
   - ☐ c. enjoys meeting people.

More Spelling Power to You

Look closely at the ten boldface words in the passage. Write each word in a sentence and underline the spelling word. Study the words (see page 103). Then complete the spelling check on the next page. It contains some words from the last lesson and most of the words from this lesson. Therefore, you must review all of the words you have learned before you complete the exercise. Concentrate on words that you previously misspelled.

Check Your Spelling Power

Underline the misspelled word in each sentence. Then write the word correctly on the line provided.

____________________ 1. The first time I went ice-skating, I felt a bit awkward, but after a while it was actualy quite pleasant.

____________________ 2. Although everyone appreciated your help, Glen certainly benefitted most from your assistance.

____________________ 3. Do you believe that a daily program of phisical fitness is really important?

____________________ 4. The polar bear has great strenth and can move swiftly when the occasion demands it.

____________________ 5. We became conscious of the fact that the cat had a mysterious smile on its face, and that the canary, evidentally, was missing.

____________________ 6. The excitement in the air was definitly noticeable.

____________________ 7. Do not despair; the problem will eventually be solved by sience.

____________________ 8. When they were younger they were almost always together, but now they have gone their seperate ways.

____________________ 9. The newspaper report refered to her as "a courageous person."

____________________ 10. When you do not posess good health, you recognize its importance.

Check your answers in the answer key on page 99. In your notebook, keep a list of the words you misspelled. Study those words until you master them.

Words Often Confused and Misused

Carefully study the meanings of the words and the sample sentences. Complete the exercise below by writing *right* and *write* in the proper blanks.

right The word *right* means "correct or good." It may also mean "the direction that is opposite of left."

write The word *write* means "to form words or letters, usually with a pencil or pen."

You were **right** to turn **right** at the corner.
How many plays did Shakespeare **write**?
You will not be able to **write** to me if you do not have the **right** address.

1. Please __________ once a week so that we know you're all __________.
2. After you figure out the __________ answer, __________ the solution in the box on the __________.
3. When you __________ to your senator, explain why you think you are __________.

Now review the Words Often Confused and Misused from lessons 1–24. They will be included in the Cumulative Review that begins on the next page.

Cumulative Review of Units 1–6

A. In each of the following groups of words, one word is misspelled. Circle the misspelled word. Then write the word correctly on the line to the left.

______________ 1. hurryng
science
describe

______________ 2. recieve
possess
scene

______________ 3. eighth
often
pursuade

______________ 4. again
bigest
planned

______________ 5. refered
evidently
committed

______________ 6. accurate
boundery
anxious

______________ 7. argue
handkerchief
anounces

______________ 8. continually
ignorant
acommodate

______________ 9. disappear
indian
weigh

______________ 10. busness
strength
brilliant

B. Fill in the blanks in the words to create words that are spelled correctly. Then write the words on the lines to the left.

______________ 11. d _ vided

______________ 12. democra _ y

______________ 13. assist _ nce

______________ 14. satisfact _ ry

______________ 15. sens _ ble

______________ 16. sp _ _ ch

______________ 17. experi _ n _ e

______________ 18. sep _ r _ te

______________ 19. criti _ i _ m

______________ 20. ind _ p _ nd _ nt

C. The letters *ie* or *ei* are missing from each of the words below. Fill in the blanks in each word to spell the word correctly. Then write the word on the line to the left.

______________ 21. th _ _ f

______________ 22. y _ _ ld

______________ 23. w _ _ rd

______________ 24. gr _ _ ve

______________ 25. for _ _ gn

D. In each of the following sentences, one of the three underlined words is misspelled. Circle the misspelled word. Then write the word correctly on the line before the sentence.

______________ 26. I <u>sincerly</u> enjoy <u>picnicking</u> on a <u>pleasant</u> day.

______________ 27. At the <u>beginning</u> of the book, the <u>author</u> states her reasons for <u>writting</u> the novel.

_______________ 28. The captain was responsable for carrying out the mission.

_______________ 29. The balloon began to discend slowly, and finally it dropped into the ocean.

_______________ 30. Do you have an explanation for that mysterious occurence?

_______________ 31. I shall always be gratefull for the college education that has benefited me so much.

_______________ 32. When we heard that you were coming to town, we immediatly made plans to visit.

_______________ 33. James will succeed as a comic because his humerous style is really delightful.

_______________ 34. Somehow, he was able to persuade an aquaintance to take part in his silly scheme.

_______________ 35. Good literature can actually make an imagnary world seem real.

E. Each of the following sentences contains two words in parentheses. Underline the one that makes the sentence correct. Then write the word on the line to the left.

_______________ 36. We were just talking about how quickly the summer (past, passed).

_______________ 37. Henry Clay once said, "I would rather be (right, write) than be president."

_______________ 38. He found it easier to (accept, except) praise than responsibility.

_______________ 39. The insurance company did not consider the accident (miner, minor).

_______________ 40. After they were (shone, shown) the house, they decided to buy it.

_______________ 41. In a famous play, Polonius offers his son some (advice, advise).

_______________ 42. If you (loose, lose) your way, blow this whistle and we'll find you.

_______________ 43. It's not a question of the money; it's a matter of (principal, principle).

_______________ 44. The three wise monkeys could (hear, here) no evil, see no evil, and speak no evil.

_______________ 45. Do you know (whose, who's) twenty dollar bill this is?

_______________ 46. It is often a good idea to (right, write) about people and things you know best.

_______________ 47. Perhaps I'll have another (peace, piece) of pie after all.

_______________ 48. The lessons of the (past, passed) can help us in the future.

_______________ 49. I hope that my (knew, new) friends will be my old friends one day.

_______________ 50. I know (your, you're) doing well on this exercise.

Unit 7

Olympic Feats

When you have completed this unit, you will have mastered 280 of the words that are most frequently misspelled and 58 words that are commonly confused and misused.

Check Your Reading POWER

Athletes from around the globe gather in a **different** country every four years to participate in the Olympic Games.

The Games give athletes an **opportunity** to compete in the spirit of friendship and peace. Each **athlete** knows that it is an honor, as well as a responsibility, to be a **representative** of his or her country.

During ceremonies that **precede** the Games, the participants **pledge obedience** to the rules of sportsmanship and fair play.

The Olympic Games are divided into two parts. The Summer Olympics feature track and field events, while the Winter Olympics <u>highlight</u> **skiing** and skating. Some other Olympic sports are boxing, wrestling, hockey, **swimming,** and **bicycle** racing.

Put an X in the box next to the correct answer. After you have completed the exercise, check your answers.

Pick the Main Idea

1. This selection is mainly about
   - ☐ a. the Summer Olympics.
   - ☐ b. ceremonies at the Olympics.
   - ☐ c. the Olympic Games.

Observe Supporting Details

2. The Olympic Games are held
   - ☐ a. every two years.
   - ☐ b. every four years.
   - ☐ c. in a different country every year.

Watch for New Vocabulary

3. As used in this selection, what is the meaning of the word <u>highlight</u>?
   - ☐ a. shadow or shade
   - ☐ b. slip or fall
   - ☐ c. feature or spotlight

Explain Cause and Effect

4. Which sentence best explains why the Games are held?
   - ☐ a. The Games give athletes a chance to become famous.
   - ☐ b. The Games give athletes a chance to compete in an atmosphere of friendship and fair play.
   - ☐ c. The Games give athletes a chance to travel around the globe.

Read to Draw Inferences

5. We may infer that the Winter Olympics must be held in a country that
   - ☐ a. has ski slopes.
   - ☐ b. is very warm.
   - ☐ c. has the best skiers.

More Spelling Power to You

Look closely at the ten boldface words in the passage. Write each word in a sentence and underline the spelling word. Study the words (see page 103). Then complete the spelling check on the next page. It contains some words from the last lesson and most of the words from this lesson. Therefore, you must review all of the words you have learned before you complete the exercise. Concentrate on words that you previously misspelled.

Check Your Spelling Power

In each group of words, one word is misspelled. On the line, write the letter of the misspelled word.

	a.	b.	c.
1. ______	a. swiming	b. running	c. million
2. ______	a. pledge	b. sieze	c. almost
3. ______	a. remember	b. interrupt	c. preceed
4. ______	a. flys	b. skiing	c. definitely
5. ______	a. character	b. athalete	c. thoroughly
6. ______	a. bycycle	b. individual	c. eleventh
7. ______	a. absolutely	b. obediance	c. physical
8. ______	a. representative	b. drownd	c. privilege
9. ______	a. diffrent	b. marriage	c. attempt
10. ______	a. transferred	b. realize	c. oportunity

Check your answers in the answer key on page 100. In your notebook, keep a list of the words you misspelled. Study those words until you master them.

Words Often Confused and Misused

Carefully study the meanings of the words and the sample sentences. Complete the exercise below by writing *desert* and *dessert* in the proper blanks.

desert The noun *desert* (DEZ-ert) means "a dry area or region." The verb *desert* (dih-ZERT) means "to abandon or leave."

dessert The noun *dessert* (dih-ZERT) means "the last course at a meal." (Some people say that you add a second *s* because you always want *more* dessert.)

Fortunately, their guide did not **desert** them in the middle of the **desert.**
He ate so much of the main course that he could barely touch his **dessert.**
She decided to **desert** her diet and order **dessert.**

1. At the edge of the ______________ was a store where you could buy sandwiches and ______________.

2. Nothing is as refreshing as a cool ______________ in the blazing ______________.

3. He planned to ______________ his family and go off to live alone in the ______________.

Now review the Words Often Confused and Misused from previous lessons. They will be included in the Cumulative Review that follows lesson 32.

Lesson 26

Check Your Reading POWER

Who would have thought that a girl who could not walk as a child would **develop** into a world-class runner?

When she was only four years old, Wilma Rudolph was stricken with a terrible disease. She lost the use of one leg, and doctors could not **guarantee** that she would ever walk again. After a **siege** of more than three years, young Wilma was **finally** able to walk properly.

Wilma began to **exercise** regularly. She also participated in sports as often as **possible.** One day while she was playing basketball in high school, a coach noticed that Wilma could run like **lightning.** He suggested she take up track, which she did, with amazing **success.**

Before long, Wilma was a star. In the 1960 Olympics, at the age of twenty, she won three gold medals—the most any American woman had ever won in track. Because of her talent and **shining** personality, no one could please a **crowd** the way Wilma Rudolph could.

Put an X in the box next to the correct answer. After you have completed the exercise, check your answers.

Pick the Main Idea

1. This selection is mainly about
   - ☐ a. the life of Wilma Rudolph.
   - ☐ b. why Wilma Rudolph played basketball.
   - ☐ c. a disease that struck Wilma Rudolph.

Observe Supporting Details

2. In the 1960 Olympics, Wilma Rudolph
   - ☐ a. won a total of two events.
   - ☐ b. won three gold medals.
   - ☐ c. was not liked by the fans.

Watch for New Vocabulary

3. What is the meaning of the word stricken?
   - ☐ a. hit
   - ☐ b. pleased
   - ☐ c. drowned

Explain Cause and Effect

4. Wilma Rudolph took up track because
   - ☐ a. a coach suggested that she try it.
   - ☐ b. her family thought she might win some medals.
   - ☐ c. her friends said she could run like lightning.

Read to Draw Inferences

5. This story suggests that
   - ☐ a. Wilma Rudolph was the world's greatest athlete.
   - ☐ b. Wilma's disease was not serious.
   - ☐ c. it is sometimes possible to turn a weakness into a strength.

More Spelling Power to You

Look closely at the ten boldface words in the passage. Write each word in a sentence and underline the spelling word. Study the words (see page 103). Then complete the spelling check on the next page. It contains some words from the last lesson and most of the words from this lesson. Therefore, you must review all of the words you have learned before you complete the exercise. Concentrate on words that you previously misspelled.

Check Your Spelling Power

Circle the misspelled word in each of the following pairs of words. Then write the word correctly on the line provided.

______________ 1. croud
different

______________ 2. swimming
possable

______________ 3. ansered
siege

______________ 4. shinning
ancient

______________ 5. success
speek

______________ 6. sking
lightning

______________ 7. exercize
achieve

______________ 8. guarante
athlete

______________ 9. finaly
bicycle

______________ 10. precede
develope

Check your answers in the answer key on page 100. In your notebook, keep a list of the words you misspelled. Study those words until you master them.

Words Often Confused and Misused

Carefully study the meanings of the words and the sample sentences. Complete the exercise below by writing *their, they're,* and *there* in the proper blanks.

their The word *their* is a possessive pronoun meaning "belonging to them."

they're The word *they're* is a contraction. It means "they are." The apostrophe takes the place of the *a* in *are.*

there The word *there* means "at or in that place."

The birds flew into **their** nest.
Remind the twins that if **they're** late they will miss the first act.
If you get **there** early, please wait for me.

1. Cats almost always land on ______________ feet; I think ______________ amazing.
2. Although ______________ the best batters on the team, ______________ always out early, practicing ______________ hitting.
3. We'll be ______________ at two o'clock sharp, so please make certain that ______________ ready.

Now review the Words Often Confused and Misused from previous lessons. They will be included in the Cumulative Review following lesson 32.

Check Your Reading POWER

The star of the 1912 Olympics was a twenty-four-year-old American Indian named Jim Thorpe. A **fierce** competitor, with blazing speed and raw power, Thorpe won the five-event pentathlon and the ten-event decathlon—an unbelievable **accomplishment.**

Ten years later, however, a **special committee** determined that Thorpe had not been **eligible** to participate in the Olympic Games. The committee **decided** that Thorpe had been a professional athlete rather than an amateur because he once had been given a small sum of **expense** money to play baseball one summer. After much **discussion,** Thorpe was stripped of his Olympic medals. His name and his victories were deleted from Olympic record books

More than fifty years later, however, the **decision** was reversed. Thorpe's medals were returned to his family, and his great feats, **omitted** for so long, are now once again part of the Olympic record.

Put an X in the box next to the correct answer. After you have completed the exercise, check your answers.

Pick the Main Idea

1. This selection is mainly about
   - ☐ a. the 1912 Olympics.
   - ☐ b. Jim Thorpe's place in Olympic history.
   - ☐ c. the family of a great Olympic athlete.

Observe Supporting Details

2. Which one of the following statements is true?
   - ☐ a. Jim Thorpe did not participate in the 1912 Olympics.
   - ☐ b. Jim Thorpe won the pentathlon and the decathlon.
   - ☐ c. In 1912, Jim Thorpe was twenty years old.

Watch for New Vocabulary

3. What is the meaning of the word deleted?
   - ☐ a. put in
   - ☐ b. taken out
   - ☐ c. questioned

Explain Cause and Effect

4. Jim Thorpe lost his Olympic medals
   - ☐ a. as the result of a committee's decision.
   - ☐ b. because he had not finished first in some events.
   - ☐ c. because of poor sportsmanship on his part.

Read to Draw Inferences

5. We may infer that the Olympic Games were open to
   - ☐ a. anyone who wishes to enter.
   - ☐ b. professional athletes only.
   - ☐ c. amateur athletes only.

More Spelling Power to You

Look closely at the ten boldface words in the passage. Write each word in a sentence and underline the spelling word. Study the words (see page 103). Then complete the spelling check on the next page. It contains some words from the last lesson and most of the words from this lesson. Therefore, you must review all of the words you have learned before you complete the exercise.

Check Your Spelling Power

Circle the misspelled word in each of the following groups of words. Then write the word correctly on the line provided.

______ 1. special
sucess
opportunity
unusual

______ 2. comittee
crowd
among
forward

______ 3. finally
dicided
complete
amusing

______ 4. guarantee
really
relief
elegible

______ 5. possible
conscience
acomplishment
schedule

______ 6. omited
skiing
noticeable
vacant

______ 7. fierce
aquire
against
immediately

______ 8. representitive
expense
generally
approach

______ 9. lieutenant
studying
develop
discusion

______ 10. exercise
system
dicision
siege

Check your answers in the answer key on page 100. In your notebook, keep a list of the words you misspelled. Study those words until you master them.

Words Often Confused and Misused

Carefully study the meanings of the words and the sample sentences. Complete the exercise below by writing *coarse* and *course* in the proper blanks.

coarse — The word *coarse* means "rough or crude."

course — The word *course* has several meanings. The most common are "a unit of study," "a path," and "part of a meal."

Although his manner seems **coarse**, he is actually quite gentle.
Sandra took an excellent **course** in auto repairs.
The golf ball hit some **coarse** sand and rolled off **course**.

1. The man in the ______ wool sweater teaches this ______.
2. The waiter's manner was so ______, we complained after he served the first ______.
3. She was removed from the ______ because of her ______ language.

Now review the Words Often Confused and Misused from previous lessons. They will be included in the Cumulative Review following lesson 32.

Lesson 28

Check Your Reading POWER

Among people who follow sports, there is general **acknowledgment** that Babe Didrikson Zaharias was America's greatest woman athlete. During her twenty-year career, there seemed to be no **ceiling** on her athletic ability. Indeed, it would be hard to **exaggerate** what she **meant** to sports.

As an all-round athlete, Babe had no **parallel.** Born Mildred Ella Didrikson, classmates used to **address** her as "Babe" because she could smash a baseball "like Babe Ruth." Babe was **built** slender and tall. She was a famous women's professional basketball player for years. She was also renowned as a track-and-field star.

In the 1932 Olympics, Babe won gold medals in the javelin throw and the 80-meter hurdles. She also won a silver medal in the high jump. A few years later, a **mischievous** rival suggested that Babe take up golf in her **leisure** time. Babe did, and she did not **disappoint** her fans. Before she retired, she won more tournaments than any woman who ever lived.

Put an X in the box next to the correct answer. After you have completed the exercise, check your answers.

Pick the Main Idea

1. This selection is mainly about
   - ☐ a. the person many people think of as America's greatest woman athlete.
   - ☐ b. some sports played in the 1932 Olympic Games.
   - ☐ c. how to become a champion at golf.

Observe Supporting Details

2. According to this selection, Babe Didrikson
   - ☐ a. was an outstanding swimmer.
   - ☐ b. played professional baseball.
   - ☐ c. played professional basketball.

Watch for New Vocabulary

3. What is the meaning of the word renowned?
   - ☐ a. new
   - ☐ b. famous
   - ☐ c. swift

Explain Cause and Effect

4. Babe Didrikson was called "Babe" because
   - ☐ a. she asked her classmates to call her by that name.
   - ☐ b. she could hit a baseball like Babe Ruth.
   - ☐ c. her family liked the name.

Read to Draw Inferences

5. If Babe had played tennis, she would probably have
   - ☐ a. played poorly.
   - ☐ b. become an outstanding player.
   - ☐ c. disliked the sport.

More Spelling Power to You

Look closely at the ten boldface words in the passage. Write each word in a sentence and underline the spelling word. Study the words (see page 103). Then complete the spelling check on the next page. It contains some words from the last lesson and most of the words from this lesson. Therefore, you must review all of the words you have learned before you complete the exercise.

Check Your Spelling Power

Underline the misspelled word in each sentence. Then write the word correctly on the line provided.

_______________ 1. After much discussion, they decided to paint the cieling blue.

_______________ 2. The committee did excellent work; however, you should not exagerate its importance.

_______________ 3. I meant to thank you for going to such great expence, but in the excitement I forgot.

_______________ 4. His mischievious manner will probably get him into trouble occasionally.

_______________ 5. Roberta's main accomplishment was the beautiful art work she did in her liesure time.

_______________ 6. Every athlete, naturally, hopes not to disapoint the fans.

_______________ 7. I am familiar with both roads; they are paralell to each other and are approximately five miles apart.

_______________ 8. The house was built without windows; therfore it is not possible for the sun to shine in.

_______________ 9. When you adress the crowd, it is necessary to speak in a loud voice.

_______________ 10. We were glad to see you finally receive the aknowledgment you deserve.

Check your answers in the answer key on page 100. In your notebook, keep a list of the words you misspelled. Study those words until you master them.

Words Often Confused and Misused

Carefully study the meanings of the words and the sample sentences. Complete the exercise below by writing *know* and *no* in the proper blanks.

know The word *know* means "to have knowledge or facts."

no The word *no* means "not at all" or "not any."

Do you **know** how many moons Jupiter has?
I am sorry to have to say **no** to your request.
Mr. Leung is **no** longer here; I do not **know** his new address.

1. Since Andrea is __________ better, her mother does not __________ when she will be able to return to school.

2. I do not __________ if we can make a substitution, because we have __________ time-outs left.

3. There is __________ way I will be able to __________ all the information by tomorrow.

Now review the Words Often Confused and Misused from previous lessons. They will be included in the Cumulative Review following lesson 32.

Unit 8

Safety First

When you have completed this unit, you will have mastered 320 of the words that are most frequently misspelled and 66 words that are commonly confused and misused.

Lesson 29

Check Your Reading POWER

Do you know that the kitchen is probably the most **dangerous** room in your house? According to surveys, more **serious** injuries occur there than anywhere else in the home.

Here are a few tips that experts on **safety recommend** to help you **guard** against accidents in the kitchen. First, water and electricity don't mix. Therefore, it is imperative that you keep electrical appliances from getting wet. It is also important to keep napkins and papers off the stove and to turn the handles of pots and pans on the stove inward.

Make sure that **knife** blades are well sharpened. A dull knife is more **likely** to slip and cause injury. When using a knife, cut away from yourself rather than toward yourself. And don't use water to try to put out an oil or a grease fire. Water will only spread the flames.

Here is one last **suggestion:** Keep a fire extinguisher handy. But if a fire gets out of **control,** do not **endeavor** to combat it. Leave at once and get help.

Put an X in the box next to the correct answer. After you have completed the exercise, check your answers.

Pick the Main Idea

1. This selection is mainly about
   - ☐ a. how to prevent accidents in the kitchen.
   - ☐ b. why a dull knife is likely to cause an injury.
   - ☐ c. how to respond to an emergency.

Observe Supporting Details

2. According to the passage, if a fire gets out of control, you should
   - ☐ a. try to fight it.
   - ☐ b. go to another room.
   - ☐ c. leave at once.

Watch for New Vocabulary

3. As used in this selection, the word imperative means
   - ☐ a. very important.
   - ☐ b. not necessary.
   - ☐ c. quite funny.

Explain Cause and Effect

4. Throwing water on a grease fire will
   - ☐ a. put out the fire at once.
   - ☐ b. put out the fire after a while.
   - ☐ c. spread the flames.

Read to Draw Inferences

5. Why should the handles of pots and pans be turned inward?
   - ☐ a. Foods cook better that way.
   - ☐ b. They are less likely to be knocked into.
   - ☐ c. You will have more room on the stove.

More Spelling Power to You

Look closely at the ten boldface words in the passage. Write each word in a sentence and underline the spelling word. Study the words (see page 103). Then complete the spelling check on the next page. It contains some words from the last lesson and most of the words from this lesson. Therefore, you must review all of the words you have learned before you complete the exercise.

Check Your Spelling Power

In each group of words, one word is misspelled. On the line, write the letter of the misspelled word.

	a.	b.	c.
1. ________	a. omitted	b. safty	c. address
2. ________	a. likly	b. eligible	c. accidentally
3. ________	a. ceiling	b. exceed	c. sugestion
4. ________	a. guard	b. chief	c. feirce
5. ________	a. exaggerate	b. controll	c. bicycle
6. ________	a. serious	b. bilt	c. restaurant
7. ________	a. parallel	b. ambition	c. dangerus
8. ________	a. recomend	b. mischievous	c. having
9. ________	a. seige	b. knife	c. neither
10. ________	a. leisure	b. opinion	c. endevor

Check your answers in the answer key on page 100. In your notebook, keep a list of the words you misspelled. Study those words until you master them.

Words Often Confused and Misused

Carefully study the meanings of the words and the sample sentences. Complete the exercise below by writing *capital* and *capitol* in the proper blanks.

capital The word *capital* means "a place where a seat of government is located." Sentences and proper names also begin with *capital* letters.

capitol The word *capitol* means "a government building in which the legislature of a state or country meets."

Paris, the **capital** of France, begins with a **capital** letter.
The roof of the **capitol** is made of marble.
In Albany, the **capital** of New York, we met with a senator in the halls of the **capitol**.

1. When Letitia was in Sacramento, the ________________ of California, she had lunch in the cafeteria at the ________________.
2. Washington, D.C., the ________________ of the United States, must always be written with a ________________ letter.
3. The ________________ is in the center of the city; it is the most striking building in the ________________.

Now review the Words Often Confused and Misused from previous lessons. They will be included in the Cumulative Review following lesson 32.

Check Your Reading POWER

Seat belts save lives. According to a **government bulletin,** if every driver and passenger buckled up, more than five thousand traffic deaths would be prevented each year.

Still, some people refuse to wear seat belts. What is the reason for their **prejudice** against seat belts?

A common excuse is that seat belts are not **comfortable**—that they are a **hindrance** to movement. Of course, broken bones are far more uncomfortable, and you can't move at all when you are in a **cemetery.**

Some people offer the **argument** that it is safer to be thrown from the car in the event of a crash. People who believe that **deceive** themselves. Being thrown from a car is twenty-five times more <u>lethal</u> than being held in place by a seat belt.

So the next time you are in an auto, use your **intelligence** and **knowledge**. Buckle up! Seat belts are good for your health.

Put an X in the box next to the correct answer. After you have completed the exercise, check your answers.

Pick the Main Idea

1. This selection is mainly about
   - ☐ a. a government bulletin.
   - ☐ b. an argument against buckling up.
   - ☐ c. the importance of wearing a seat belt.

Observe Supporting Details

2. Being thrown from a car in a crash is
   - ☐ a. about as dangerous as being held in the car by a seat belt.
   - ☐ b. less dangerous than being held in the car by a seat belt.
   - ☐ c. much more dangerous than being held in the car by a seat belt.

Watch for New Vocabulary

3. What is the meaning of the word <u>lethal</u>?
   - ☐ a. upsetting
   - ☐ b. deadly
   - ☐ c. restricting

Explain Cause and Effect

4. If all drivers and passengers wore seat belts,
   - ☐ a. thousands of lives would be saved each year.
   - ☐ b. there would be many more traffic deaths each year.
   - ☐ c. the number of traffic deaths would remain about the same.

Read to Draw Inferences

5. Some people say that wearing seat belts is uncomfortable. The passage suggests that this argument is
   - ☐ a. excellent.
   - ☐ b. foolish.
   - ☐ c. wise.

More Spelling Power to You

Look closely at the ten boldface words in the passage. Write each word in a sentence and underline the spelling word. Study the words (see page 103). Then complete the spelling check on the next page. It contains some words from the last lesson and most of the words from this lesson. Therefore, you must review all of the words you have learned before you complete the exercise. Concentrate on words that you previously misspelled.

Check Your Spelling Power

Circle the misspelled word in each of the following pairs of words. Then write the word correctly on the line provided.

________	1. knowledge serius	________	6. hinderance control
________	2. comftable cafeteria	________	7. suggestion cemetary
________	3. arguement pledge	________	8. intellagence dependent
________	4. different goverment	________	9. predjudice disappoint
________	5. decieve recommend	________	10. acknowledgment buletin

Check your answers in the answer key on page 100. In your notebook, keep a list of the words you misspelled. Study those words until you master them.

Words Often Confused and Misused

Carefully study the meanings of the words and the sample sentences. Complete the exercise below by writing *choose* and *chose* in the proper blanks.

choose — The word *choose* means "select or pick." Notice that *choose* shows either the present or the future tense.

chose — The word *chose* means "selected or picked." *Chose* is the past tense of *choose*.

Please choose your partner for the dance.
Yesterday we chose Manuela as treasurer.
My sister, Diane, didn't know which college to choose; finally she chose State University.

1. I'm glad I ________ this gift; which gift do you plan to ________?
2. Forced to ________ between baseball and football, Mark eventually ________ baseball.
3. If you are still unhappy with the book you ________, you may ________ another.

Now review the Words Often Confused and Misused from previous lessons. They will be included in the Cumulative Review following lesson 32.

Check Your Reading POWER

Some **laboratory** studies suggest that sitting in an airplane for many hours without moving may be bad for your health. When you sit in one place for a very long time, blood clots can develop in your legs. These clots can travel through the blood to the heart, where they are **particularly** dangerous.

Therefore, when you fly for hours, **perhaps** you should move about from time to time. Do this even if you are very **tired.** Do not feel **guilty** about requesting the passenger next to you to move. No one will think you a **villain** if you excuse yourself in a **courteous** way. Your neighbor is not likely to become angry or irritable. Walking a bit will provide the **rhythm** you need to keep your blood moving. Very few people develop clots. Still, you don't want to **sacrifice** your health during an **innocent** airplane trip.

Put an X in the box next to the correct answer. After you have completed the exercise, check your answers.

Pick the Main Idea

1. This selection is mainly about
   - ☐ a. studies made by experts on health.
   - ☐ b. why you should move about during a long airplane trip.
   - ☐ c. the reasons why people are afraid to travel by airplane.

Observe Supporting Details

2. According to the selection, if you sit in one place for a very long time, you
   - ☐ a. will bother the people around you.
   - ☐ b. will probably get very tired.
   - ☐ c. may develop blood clots in your legs.

Watch for New Vocabulary

3. Judging from the context of the sentence in which it appears, what is the meaning of the word irritable?
   - ☐ a. annoyed
   - ☐ b. happy
   - ☐ c. calm

Explain Cause and Effect

4. When clots travel to the heart, they
   - ☐ a. never cause any problems.
   - ☐ b. can be very harmful.
   - ☐ c. make the heart stronger.

Read to Draw Inferences

5. This article suggests that
   - ☐ a. haste makes waste.
   - ☐ b. it is better to be safe than sorry.
   - ☐ c. things are seldom what they seem to be.

More Spelling Power to You

Look closely at the ten boldface words in the passage. Write each word in a sentence and underline the spelling word. Study the words (see page 103). Then complete the spelling check on the next page. It contains some words from the last lesson and most of the words from this lesson. Therefore, you must review all of the words you have learned before you complete the exercise. Concentrate on words that you previously misspelled.

Check Your Spelling Power

Circle the misspelled word in each of the following groups of words. Then write the word correctly on the line provided.

______ 1. government
guard
terrible
inocent

______ 2. tired
knive
intelligence
likely

______ 3. labratory
hindrance
dangerous
disagreeable

______ 4. bulletin
fortunately
rythm
special

______ 5. cemetery
gilty
swimming
preferred

______ 6. purhaps
prejudice
committee
hesitate

______ 7. permanent
meant
sacrafice
endeavor

______ 8. parallel
unnecessary
shriek
villian

______ 9. comfortable
paticularly
preparation
expense

______ 10. argument
quantity
courtious
sufficient

Check your answers in the answer key on page 100. In your notebook, keep a list of the words you misspelled. Study those words until you master them.

Words Often Confused and Misused

Carefully study the meanings of the words and the sample sentences. Complete the exercise below by writing *plain* and *plane* in the proper blanks.

plain The word *plain* means "simple or easy." It may also refer to "a prairie, or flat and level piece of land."

plane The word *plane* has several meanings. The most common are "an airplane" and "a tool used for smoothing or shaping wood."

The pioneers who lived on the **plain** were used to eating **plain** meals.
In wood shop, Gwen used a **plane** to smooth the wings of the **plane** she had built.
The **plane** flew high above the **plain**.

1. The carpenter always wore a ______ apron to keep the shavings from the ______ away from his clothing.

2. Looking down from the ______, we could clearly see the outlines of a large, green ______.

3. The pilot used clear, ______ language to discuss the teamwork necessary to fly a large jet ______.

Now review the Words Often Confused and Misused from previous lessons. They will be included in the Cumulative Review following lesson 32.

Lesson 32

Check Your Reading POWER

One should never travel in the desert without plenty of water. Several years ago, two young men **practically** lost their lives when they forgot that rule of safety.

Their problems began when their car got stuck in the soft sand of the Mojave Desert. Since the auto **stopped** just short of a hard gravel road, they began to push the car, **hoping** to reach the road.

The sun, however, blazed down with a **vengeance,** creating **awful** heat. One man passed out and the other grew dizzy. Luckily, however, the second man had an idea. He drained some water from the car's radiator and drank the precious liquid. Repeating the **procedure,** he obtained some water for his **friend.** The water made the **difference.** Once refreshed, they had enough strength to get the car onto the road. After several **tries** at starting the car, the men got the motor to turn over, and they continued their journey.

In **summary:** one should always take water along when traveling in the desert.

Put an X in the box next to the correct answer. After you have completed the exercise, check your answers.

Pick the Main Idea

1. This selection is mainly about
   - ☐ a. why a car got stuck in the desert.
   - ☐ b. several rules of safety to follow when traveling.
   - ☐ c. how water saved the lives of two men in the desert.

Observe Supporting Details

2. The car came to a halt
   - ☐ a. not far from a road.
   - ☐ b. many miles from a road.
   - ☐ c. on a hard gravel road.

Watch for New Vocabulary

3. What is the meaning of the word refreshed?
   - ☐ a. to exhaust or make tired
   - ☐ b. to make fresh again
   - ☐ c. to cause sadness or sorrow

Explain Cause and Effect

4. One man passed out because he
   - ☐ a. was hungry.
   - ☐ b. had been ill.
   - ☐ c. couldn't take the heat.

Read to Draw Inferences

5. The car's motor probably didn't turn over right away because
   - ☐ a. the car was almost out of gas.
   - ☐ b. it was a very old car.
   - ☐ c. the car was very hot.

More Spelling Power to You

Look closely at the ten boldface words in the passage. Write each word in a sentence and underline the spelling word. Study the words (see page 103). Then complete the spelling check on the next page. It contains some words from the last lesson and most of the words from this lesson. Therefore, you must review all of the words you have learned before you complete the exercise.

Check Your Spelling Power

Underline the misspelled word in each sentence. Then write the word correctly on the line provided.

_______________ 1. A frend is someone who is truly willing to make a sacrifice for you.

_______________ 2. One day in his laboratory, Dr. Frankenstein created an awfull and extraordinary creature.

_______________ 3. After several tries, we eventually met with the reprasentative.

_______________ 4. The dangerous villain was seeking vengance.

_______________ 5. I am hopeing to visit Montreal during Easter vacation, since that city is particularly beautiful in the spring.

_______________ 6. If you follow a different proceedure, perhaps you will have better results.

_______________ 7. The teacher said, "It is your responsibility to develop a thoughtful sumary."

_______________ 8. My heart nearly stoped beating when I heard that you had had a serious accident while skiing.

_______________ 9. In the courtroom, practicaly everyone had an opinion about whether the defendant was innocent or guilty.

_______________ 10. Let me take this opportunity to offer a suggestion: always remember that you *can* make a diffrence.

Check your answers in the answer key on page 100. In your notebook, keep a list of the words you misspelled. Study those words until you master them.

Words Often Confused and Misused

Carefully study the meanings of the words and the sample sentences. Complete the exercise below by writing *hole* and *whole* in the proper blanks.

hole The word *hole* means "an open or hollow place."

whole The word *whole* means "entire or complete."

Who first put the **hole** in the middle of the doughnut?
It was a struggle, but I finished the **whole** meal.
Mike spent the **whole** day digging a **hole** for the pool.

1. Bea missed a __________ week of school after she tripped in a __________ and sprained her ankle.

2. A large __________ in your jacket can ruin your __________ suit.

3. Our lawyer's __________ argument was so strong they could not find a __________ in the case.

Now review the Words Often Confused and Misused from lessons 1–32. They will be included in the Cumulative Review that begins on the next page.

Cumulative Review of Units 1–8

A. In each of the following groups of words, one word is misspelled. Circle the misspelled word. Then write the word correctly on the line to the left.

______ 1. biginning
lightning
villain

______ 2. government
liberary
college

______ 3. shining
address
ocurr

______ 4. suprise
happened
precede

______ 5. control
decieve
stopped

______ 6. procedure
dissappoint
sense

______ 7. prejudice
ommitted
interesting

______ 8. bulletin
rhythm
ocassion

______ 9. writen
argument
guard

______ 10. sincerely
acomodate
acknowledgment

B. Fill in the blanks in the words to create words that are spelled correctly. Then write the words on the lines to the left.

______ 11. d __ spair

______ 12. nonsen __ e

______ 13. obedi __ nce

______ 14. d __ cided

______ 15. p __ rsuade

______ 16. sep __ r __ te

______ 17. cem __ t __ ry

______ 18. criti __ i __ m

______ 19. intell __ g __ n __ e

______ 20. r __ spons __ b __ l __ ty

C. The letters *ie* or *ei* are missing from each of the words below. Fill in the blanks in each word to spell the word correctly. Then write the word on the line to the left.

______ 21. f __ __ rce

______ 22. dec __ __ ve

______ 23. ach __ __ ve

______ 24. c __ __ ling

______ 25. s __ __ ge

D. In each of the following sentences, one of the three underlined words is misspelled. Circle the misspelled word. Then write the word correctly on the line before the sentence.

______ 26. It is true that <u>succes</u> is <u>often</u> <u>built</u> on pride and hard work.

______ 27. By law, a person is considered <u>innocent</u> <u>untill</u> proven <u>guilty</u>.

______ 28. Joellyn <u>trys</u> to <u>exercise</u> twenty minutes a day during her <u>leisure</u> time.

_______________ 29. These heroes were willing to sacrifise their lives for the safety of others.

_______________ 30. A pleasant and curteous manner can make a difference when you are applying for a job.

_______________ 31. Can someone, perhaps, attempt to give you the homework during your abcense?

_______________ 32. The garantee on the equipment covered practically everything.

_______________ 33. I recommend that you try writeing another summary.

_______________ 34. Her decision was definitely based on knowlege of the facts.

_______________ 35. Be careful—our mischevous friend is likely to play a trick on us.

E. Each of the following sentences contains two or three words in parentheses. Underline the one that makes the sentence correct. Then write the word on the line to the left.

_______________ 36. It is hard to put a square peg into a round (hole, whole).

_______________ 37. Robinson Crusoe lived for years on a (desert, dessert) island.

_______________ 38. In 1927, Charles Lindbergh flew a (plain, plane) from New York to Paris.

_______________ 39. Do you (know, no) the correct word for this sentence?

_______________ 40. A Greek philosopher said, "Of evils we must (choose, chose) the least."

_______________ 41. Have you ever been to Madrid, the (capital, capitol) of Spain?

_______________ 42. Every June, our (principal, principle) wishes the graduating class good luck.

_______________ 43. Beware of tigers when (their, they're, there) hungry.

_______________ 44. As you learned earlier, snakes have (know, no) ears.

_______________ 45. You can relax and read a book regardless of the (weather, whether).

_______________ 46. At the end of the argument, the umpire (threw, through) the player out of the game.

_______________ 47. According to Shakespeare, "The (coarse, course) of true love never did run smooth."

_______________ 48. The card said: "Let us all work for world (peace, piece)."

_______________ 49. My favorite day of the (weak, week) is Friday.

_______________ 50. There are none so deaf as those who will not (hear, here).

UNIT 1

Lesson 1

Check Your Reading POWER
1.c 2.b 3.b 4.c 5.c

Check Your Spelling Power
1.c 2.b 3.a 4.b 5.a 6.a 7.c 8.b 9.b 10.c

Words Often Confused and Misused
1. accept/except 2. except/accept
3. accept/except

Lesson 2

Check Your Reading POWER
1.c 2.c 3.a 4.a 5.b

Check Your Spelling Power
1. approach 2. occasionally 3. drowned
4. biggest 5. truly 6. weigh 7. equipped
8. usually 9. sufficient 10. surprise

Words Often Confused and Misused
1. loose/lose 2. loose/lose 3. loose/lose

Lesson 3

Check Your Reading POWER
1.a 2.b 3.a 4.b 5.a

Check Your Spelling Power
1. shriek 2. all right 3. awkward
4. nonsense 5. probably 6. flies 7. generally
8. system 9. dependent 10. making

Words Often Confused and Misused
1. threw/through 2. threw/through
3. through/threw

Lesson 4

Check Your Reading POWER
1.c 2.a 3.a 4.c 5.c

Check Your Spelling Power
1. impossible 2. explanation 3. fascinating
4. grateful 5. ache 6. dependent
7. therefore 8. absolutely 9. believe
10. necessary

Words Often Confused and Misused
1. quiet/quite 2. quite/quiet 3. quite/quiet

UNIT 2

Lesson 5

Check Your Reading POWER
1.c 2.b 3.c 4.c 5.c

Check Your Spelling Power
1.b 2.c 3.a 4.b 5.a 6.b 7.c 8.a 9.b 10.c

Words Often Confused and Misused
1. it's/its 2. it's/it's 3. its/it's

Lesson 6

Check Your Reading POWER
1.c 2.b 3.c 4.b 5.c

Check Your Spelling Power
1. describe 2. written 3. balloon 4. receive
5. accidentally 6. relief 7. excitement
8. usually 9. eventually 10. all right

Words Often Confused and Misused
1. whether/weather 2. weather/whether
3. whether/weather

Lesson 7

Check Your Reading POWER
1.c 2.b 3.a 4.a 5.c

Check Your Spelling Power
1. continually 2. across 3. using 4. conquer
5. forward 6. courageous 7. celebrate
8. preparation 9. accompany 10. occasionally

Words Often Confused and Misused
1. already/all ready 2. all ready/already
3. already/all ready

Lesson 8

Check Your Reading POWER
1.b 2.b 3.a 4.a 5.c

Check Your Spelling Power
1. attendance 2. succeed 3. familiar
4. extraordinary 5. recognize 6. occasion
7. losing 8. business 9. speak 10. exhibit

Words Often Confused and Misused
1. whose/who's 2. whose/who's 3. who's/whose

Cumulative Review of Units 1 and 2

A. 1. all right 2. equipped 3. eventually
4. forward 5. drowned 6. approach
7. business 8. generally 9. accidentally
10. nonsense

B. 11. terrible 12. discover 13. attendance
14. preparation 15. conquer 16. speak
17. impossible 18. responsible 19. dependent
20. description

C. 21. receive 22. height 23. relief 24. shriek
25. believe

D. 26. library 27. fascinating 28. excitement
29. interesting 30. surprise 31. acquire
32. straight 33. necessary 34. flies 35. occasion

E. 36. quiet 37. weather 38. already 39. its
40. through 41. who's 42. accept 43. lose
44. quite 45. threw 46. it's 47. loose
48. except 49. whose 50. whether

Answer Key

UNIT 3

Lesson 9

Check Your Reading POWER
1. b 2. b 3. c 4. a 5. b

Check Your Spelling Power
1. c 2. c 3. b 4. a 5. b 6. c 7. b 8. a 9. a 10. b

Words Often Confused and Misused
1. to/too/two 2. to/to/two/too 3. too/to/to/to/two

Lesson 10

Check Your Reading POWER
1. c 2. b 3. a 4. b 5. b

Check Your Spelling Power
1. always 2. forty 3. awkward 4. succeed
5. extraordinary 6. existence 7. interrupt
8. permitted 9. valuable 10. disagreeable

Words Often Confused and Misused
1. than/then 2. then/than 3. then/than

Lesson 11

Check Your Reading POWER
1. c 2. a 3. c 4. b 5. a

Check Your Spelling Power
1. cafeteria 2. having 3. similar 4. sandwich
5. prefer 6. naturally 7. million 8. restaurant
9. favorite 10. banquet

Words Often Confused and Misused
1. weak/week 2. week/weak/week 3. weak/week

Lesson 12

Check Your Reading POWER
1. c 2. c 3. a 4. a 5. b

Check Your Spelling Power
1. eventually 2. appreciate 3. temperature
4. Indian 5. relief 6. extremely 7. ordinary
8. buried 9. before 10. occur

Words Often Confused and Misused
1. you're/your/you're 2. your/your/you're
3. you're/your/your

UNIT 4

Lesson 13

Check Your Reading POWER
1. b 2. a 3. b 4. c 5. b

Check Your Spelling Power
1. b 2. a 3. a 4. a 5. c 6. b 7. a 8. b 9. a 10. c

Words Often Confused and Misused
1. knew/new/new 2. new/knew 3. knew/new

Lesson 14

Check Your Reading POWER
1. b 2. a 3. a 4. b 5. c

Check Your Spelling Power
1. vacant 2. twelfth 3. grateful 4. consider
5. preferred 6. surprise 7. occurrence
8. calendar 9. genuine 10. humorous

Words Often Confused and Misused
1. stationary/stationery 2. stationery/stationary
3. stationary/stationery

Lesson 15

Check Your Reading POWER
1. b 2. c 3. a 4. c 5. b

Check Your Spelling Power
1. hesitate 2. seize 3. argue 4. honorable
5. pursue 6. embarrass 7. responsibility
8. defense 9. occurred 10. exceed

Words Often Confused and Misused
1. altogether/all together 2. all together/altogether
3. altogether/all together

Lesson 16

Check Your Reading POWER
1. c 2. a 3. c 4. a 5. c

Check Your Spelling Power
1. appearance 2. answered 3. occurred
4. certainly 5. doubt 6. usually 7. apologize
8. accommodate 9. approximately 10. therefore

Words Often Confused and Misused
1. brake/break 2. break/brake 3. brake/break

Cumulative Review of Units 1–4

A. 1. exceed 2. embarrass 3. quantity 4. preferred
5. humorous 6. criticism 7. opinion
8. dependent 9. judgment 10. accommodate

B. 11. describe 12. consider 13. appearance
14. existence 15. excellent 16. apologize
17. cafeteria 18. approximately 19. permanent
20. responsibility

C. 21. chief 22. neither 23. seize
24. believe 25. weigh

D. 26. honorable 27. schedule 28. flies 29. until
30. truly 31. temperature 32. receive
33. speak 34. all right 35. although

E. 36. new 37. your 38. week 39. than
40. it's 41. too 42. whether 43. all ready
44. stationery 45. quiet 46. accept
47. break 48. whose 49. lose 50. through

UNIT 5

Lesson 17

Check Your Reading POWER
1. c 2. b 3. c 4. a 5. b

Check Your Spelling Power
1. b 2. b 3. c 4. a 5. a 6. a 7. c 8. b 9. b 10. a

Words Often Confused and Misused
1. hear/here 2. here/hear 3. hear/here

Lesson 18

Check Your Reading POWER
1. b 2. a 3. c 4. a 5. c

Check Your Spelling Power
1. writing 2. independent 3. paid 4. remember 5. heroes 6. democracy 7. vacuum 8. especially 9. existence 10. absence

Words Often Confused and Misused
1. shone/shown 2. shown/shone 3. shone/shown

Lesson 19

Check Your Reading POWER
1. b 2. b 3. c 4. a 5. b

Check Your Spelling Power
1. amusing 2. literature 3. author 4. announces 5. conscience 6. fascinating 7. ignorant 8. sensible 9. committed 10. character

Words Often Confused and Misused
1. peace/piece 2. piece/peace 3. piece/peace

Lesson 20

Check Your Reading POWER
1. a 2. c 3. a 4. c 5. b

Check Your Spelling Power
1. thief 2. marriage 3. despair 4. interesting 5. sincerely 6. disappear 7. beautiful 8. descend 9. grieve 10. judgment

Words Often Confused and Misused
1. advise/advice 2. advise/advice 3. advice/advise

UNIT 6

Lesson 21

Check Your Reading POWER
1. c 2. b 3. b 4. c 5. a

Check Your Spelling Power
1. b 2. a 3. c 4. a 5. b 6. b 7. b 8. a 9. c 10. b

Words Often Confused and Misused
1. principal/principal 2. principle/principal 3. principal/principle

Lesson 22

Check Your Reading POWER
1. a 2. b 3. a 4. c 5. a

Check Your Spelling Power
1. ancient 2. divided 3. immediately 4. truly 5. scheme 6. privilege 7. eighth 8. tragedy 9. transferred 10. individual

Words Often Confused and Misused
1. passed/past 2. past/passed 3. past/passed

Lesson 23

Check Your Reading POWER
1. a 2. c 3. b 4. b 5. c

Check Your Spelling Power
1. really 2. almost 3. captain 4. conscious 5. thoroughly 6. assistance 7. achieve 8. carrying 9. pleasant 10. noticeable

Words Often Confused and Misused
1. miner/minor 2. minor/minor 3. miner/minor

Lesson 24

Check Your Reading POWER
1. c 2. a 3. b 4. c 5. b

Check Your Spelling Power
1. actually 2. benefited 3. physical 4. strength 5. evidently 6. definitely 7. science 8. separate 9. referred 10. possess

Words Often Confused and Misused
1. write/right 2. right/write/right 3. write/right

Cumulative Review of Units 1–6

A. 1. hurrying 2. receive 3. persuade 4. biggest 5. referred 6. boundary 7. announces 8. accommodate 9. Indian 10. business

B. 11. divided 12. democracy 13. assistance 14. satisfactory 15. sensible 16. speech 17. experience 18. separate 19. criticism 20. independent

C. 21. thief 22. yield 23. weird 24. grieve 25. foreign

D. 26. sincerely 27. writing 28. responsible 29. descend 30. occurrence 31. grateful 32. immediately 33. humorous 34. acquaintance 35. imaginary

E. 36. passed 37. right 38. accept 39. minor 40. shown 41. advice 42. lose 43. principle 44. hear 45. whose 46. write 47. piece 48. past 49. new 50. you're

Answer Key

UNIT 7

Lesson 25

Check Your Reading POWER
1. c 2. b 3. c 4. b 5. a

Check Your Spelling Power
1. a 2. b 3. c 4. a 5. b 6. a 7. b 8. b 9. a 10. c

Words Often Confused and Misused
1. desert/dessert 2. dessert/desert 3. desert/desert

Lesson 26

Check Your Reading POWER
1. a 2. b 3. a 4. a 5. c

Check Your Spelling Power
1. crowd 2. possible 3. answered 4. shining 5. speak 6. skiing 7. exercise 8. guarantee 9. finally 10. develop

Words Often Confused and Misused
1. their/they're 2. they're/they're/their 3. there/they're

Lesson 27

Check Your Reading POWER
1. b 2. b 3. b 4. a 5. c

Check Your Spelling Power
1. success 2. committee 3. decided 4. eligible 5. accomplishment 6. omitted 7. acquire 8. representative 9. discussion 10. decision

Words Often Confused and Misused
1. coarse/course 2. coarse/course 3. course/coarse

Lesson 28

Check Your Reading POWER
1. a 2. c 3. b 4. b 5. b

Check Your Spelling Power
1. ceiling 2. exaggerate 3. expense 4. mischievous 5. leisure 6. disappoint 7. parallel 8. therefore 9. address 10. acknowledgment

Words Often Confused and Misused
1. no/know 2. know/no 3. no/know

UNIT 8

Lesson 29

Check Your Reading POWER
1. a 2. c 3. a 4. c 5. b

Check Your Spelling Power
1. b 2. a 3. c 4. c 5. b 6. b 7. c 8. a 9. a 10. c

Words Often Confused and Misused
1. capital/capitol 2. capital/capital 3. capitol/capital

Lesson 30

Check Your Reading POWER
1. c 2. c 3. b 4. a 5. b

Check Your Spelling Power
1. serious 2. comfortable 3. argument 4. government 5. deceive 6. hindrance 7. cemetery 8. intelligence 9. prejudice 10. bulletin

Words Often Confused and Misused
1. chose/choose 2. choose/chose 3. chose/choose

Lesson 31

Check Your Reading POWER
1. b 2. c 3. a 4. b 5. b

Check Your Spelling Power
1. innocent 2. knife 3. laboratory 4. rhythm 5. guilty 6. perhaps 7. sacrifice 8. villain 9. particularly 10. courteous

Words Often Confused and Misused
1. plain/plane 2. plane/plain 3. plain/plane

Lesson 32

Check Your Reading POWER
1. c 2. a 3. b 4. c 5. c

Check Your Spelling Power
1. friend 2. awful 3. representative 4. vengeance 5. hoping 6. procedure 7. summary 8. stopped 9. practically 10. difference

Words Often Confused and Misused
1. whole/hole 2. hole/whole 3. whole/hole

Cumulative Review of Units 1–8

A. 1. beginning 2. library 3. occur 4. surprise 5. deceive 6. disappoint 7. omitted 8. occasion 9. written 10. accommodate

B. 11. despair 12. nonsense 13. obedience 14. decided 15. persuade 16. separate 17. cemetery 18. criticism 19. intelligence 20. responsibility

C. 21. fierce 22. deceive 23. achieve 24. ceiling 25. siege

D. 26. success 27. until 28. tries 29. sacrifice 30. courteous 31. absence 32. guarantee 33. writing 34. knowledge 35. mischievous

E. 36. hole 37. desert 38. plane 39. know 40. choose 41. capital 42. principal 43. they're 44. no 45. weather 46. threw 47. course 48. peace 49. week 50. hear

List of Words By Lesson

Lesson 1
dependent, discover, fascinating, making, receive, sense, surprise, truly, using, victim
accept/except

Lesson 2
although, approach, biggest, drowned, equipped, generally, occasionally, sufficient, weigh, usually
loose/lose

Lesson 3
all right, awkward, flies, nonsense, probably, shriek, straight, studying, system, toward
threw/through

Lesson 4
absolutely, ache, believe, explanation, grateful, impossible, necessary, terrible, therefore, unusual
quiet/quite

Lesson 5
acquire, beginning, career, description, interesting, library, responsible, succeed, until, written
its/it's

Lesson 6
accidentally, ambition, balloon, busy, describe, eventually, excitement, happened, height, relief
weather/whether

Lesson 7
accompany, across, against, celebrate, coming, conquer, continually, courageous, forward, preparation
all ready/already

Lesson 8
attendance, brilliant, business, exhibit, extraordinary, familiar, losing, occasion, recognize, speak
whose/who's

Lesson 9
always, criticism, importance, often, paid, quantity, salary, similar, soldier, valuable
to/too/two

Lesson 10
anxious, disagreeable, existence, forty, guessed, interrupt, million, permitted, sandwich, source
than/then

Lesson 11
among, banquet, cafeteria, favorite, genuine, having, naturally, prefer, restaurant, suppose
weak/week

Lesson 12
appreciate, around, before, buried, enough, extremely, Indian, occur, ordinary, temperature
your/you're

Lesson 13
attempt, chief, completely, fortunately, handkerchief, permanent, proceed, schedule, speech, unnecessary
knew/new

Lesson 14
argue, calendar, consider, eleventh, humorous, neither, occurrence, preferred, twelfth, vacant
stationary/stationery

Lesson 15
apologize, defense, embarrass, exceed, hesitate, honorable, occurred, pursue, responsibility, seize
all together/altogether

Lesson 16
accommodate, answered, appearance, approximately, certainly, doubt, excellent, fourth, judgment, opinion
brake/break

List of Words By Lesson

Lesson 17
acquaintance
college
dropped
especially
hurrying
picnicking
professor
remember
running
weird
hear/here

Lesson 18
absence
author
democracy
foreign
heroes
ignorant
independent
realize
vacuum
writing
shone/shown

Lesson 19
achieve
amusing
announces
character
committed
conscience
literature
sensible
stubborn
together
peace/piece

Lesson 20
ancient
beautiful
descend
despair
disappear
grieve
marriage
persuade
sincerely
thief
advice/advise

Lesson 21
accurate
again
boundary
carrying
equipment
experience
imaginary
lieutenant
satisfactory
tragedy
principal/principle

Lesson 22
divided
eighth
heard
immediately
individual
planned
privilege
scene
scheme
transferred
past/passed

Lesson 23
almost
assistance
captain
conscious
evidently
noticeable
pleasant
really
thoroughly
yield
miner/minor

Lesson 24
actually
benefited
definitely
mysterious
physical
possess
referred
science
separate
strength
right/write

Lesson 25
athlete
bicycle
different
obedience
opportunity
pledge
precede
representative
swimming
skiing
desert/dessert

Lesson 26
crowd
develop
exercise
finally
guarantee
lightning
possible
shining
siege
success
their/they're/there

Lesson 27
accomplishment
committe
decided
decision
discussion
eligible
expense
fierce
omitted
special
coarse/course

Lesson 28
acknowledgment
address
built
ceiling
disappoint
exaggerate
leisure
meant
mischievous
parallel
know/no

Lesson 29
control
dangerous
endeavor
guard
knife
likely
recommend
safety
serious
suggestion
capital/capitol

Lesson 30
argument
bulletin
cemetery
comfortable
deceive
government
hindrance
intelligence
knowledge
prejudice
choose/chose

Lesson 31
courteous
guilty
innocent
laboratory
particularly
perhaps
rhythm
sacrifice
tired
villain
plain/plane

Lesson 32
awful
difference
friend
hoping
practically
procedure
stopped
summary
tries
vengeance
hole/whole

Spelling Strategies

Here are some good ways to study spelling. Look them over, try them out, and pick the combination that is right for you!

- Look carefully at the word.
- Write the word over and over.
- Divide the word into its syllables.
- Identify the difficult parts of the word and focus your attention on these difficult parts when you study. For example, you might spell the word aloud, emphasizing the letters or letter combinations that give you difficulty. You might also underline the difficult parts of the word in your notebook.
- See if a spelling rule applies—or does not apply—to the word.
- Find hints or clues in the word to help you remember the correct spelling. For example, there might be a word or words within the word that will help you remember the spelling. The word *separate,* for example, contains the word *rat.* Try to find other clues of your own for troublesome words.
- Say the word, and then spell it aloud.
- Close your eyes and try to see the word in your mind.
- Test yourself by covering the word and trying to spell it. Then uncover the word and check to see if you are correct.
- Have someone test you on the words.
- Keep a list of the words that you regularly misspell or words that you have misspelled on spelling checks.
- Review all your spelling words often. (This step is a must for everyone who wants to be a good speller!)

Alphabetical List of Words

absence
absolutely
accidentally
accommodate
accompany
accomplishment
accurate
ache
achieve
acknowledgment
acquaintance
acquire
across
actually
address
again
against
all right
almost
although
always
ambition
among
amusing
ancient
announces
answered
anxious
apology
appearance
appreciate
approach
approximately
argue
argument
around
assistance
athlete
attempt
attendance
author
awful
awkward
balloon
banquet
beautiful
before
beginning
believe
benefited
bicycle
biggest
boundary
brilliant
built
bulletin
buried
business
busy
cafeteria
calendar
captain
career
carrying
ceiling
celebrate
cemetery
certainly
character
chief
college
comfortable
coming
committed
committee
complete
conquer
conscience
conscious
consider
continually
control
courageous
courteous
criticism
crowd
dangerous
deceive
decided
decision
defense
definitely
democracy
dependent
descend
describe
description
despair
develop
difference
different
disagreeable
disappear
disappoint
discover
discussion
divided
doubt
dropped
drowned
eighth
eleventh
eligible
embarrass
endeavor
enough
equipment
equipped
especially
eventually
evidently
exaggerate
exceed
excellent
excitement
exercise
exhibit
existence
expense
experience
explanation
extraordinary
extremely
familiar
fascinating
favorite
fierce
finally
flies
foreign
fortunately
forty
forward
fourth
friend
generally
genuine
government
grateful
grieve
guarantee
guard
guessed
guilty
handkerchief
happened
having
heard
height
heroes
hesitate
hindrance
honorable
hoping
humorous
hurrying
ignorant
imaginary
immediately
importance
impossible
independent
Indian
individual
innocent
intelligence
interesting
interrupt
judgment
knife
knowledge
laboratory
leisure
library
lieutenant
lightning
likely
literature
losing
making
marriage
meant
million
mischievous
mysterious
naturally
necessary
neither
nonsense
noticeable
obedience
occasion
occasionally
occur
occurred
occurrence
often
omitted
opinion
opportunity
ordinary
paid
parallel
particularly
perhaps
permanent
permitted
persuade
physical
picnicking
planned
pleasant
pledge
possess
possible
practically
precede
prefer
preferred
prejudice
preparation
privilege
probably
procedure
proceed
professor
pursue
quantity
realize
really
receive
recognize
recommend
referred
relief
remember
representative
responsibility
responsible
restaurant
rhythm
running
sacrifice
safety
salary
sandwich
satisfactory
scene
schedule
scheme
science
seize
sense
sensible
separate
serious
shining
shriek
siege
similar
sincerely
skiing
soldier
source
speak
special
speech
stopped
straight
strength
stubborn
studying
succeed
success
sufficient
suggestion
summary
suppose
surprise
swimming
system
temperature
terrible
therefore
thief
thoroughly
tired
together
toward
tragedy
transferred
tries
truly
twelfth
unnecessary
until
unusual
using
usually
vacant
vacuum
valuable
vengeance
victim
villain
weigh
weird
writing
written
yield

Words Commonly Confused and Misused

accept/except
loose/lose
threw/through
quiet/quite
its/it's
weather/whether
all ready/already
whose/who's
to/too/two
than/then
weak/week
your/you're
knew/new
stationary/stationery
all together/altogether
brake/break
hear/here
shone/shown
peace/piece
advice/advise
principal/principle
past/passed
miner/minor
right/write
desert/dessert
their/they're/there
coarse/course
know/no
capital/capitol
choose/chose
plain/plane
hole/whole